P9-CQE-072

BUSINESS WITHOUT ECONOMISTS

BUSINESS WITHOUT ECONOMISTS

An Irreverent Guide

William J. Hudson

amacom

American Management Association

Library of Congress Cataloging-in-Publication Data

Hudson, W. J.
    Business without economists.

    Includes index.
    1. Business forecasting. 2. Economic forecasting.
3. Economists. I. Title.
HB3730.H83   1987   658.4'0355   86-47812
ISBN 0-8144-5896-3

Printing number

10 9 8 7 6 5 4 3 2 1

Contents

BUSINESS WITHOUT ECONOMISTS

Introduction

Business leaders routinely make more reliable forecasts than paid economists do. Many other people besides business leaders are also good at forecasting, and their forecasts are almost always better than the ones made by "experts," especially when the experts work in large teams and use the latest, most sophisticated computers.

In other words, economics doesn't work. The evidence appears daily. Economic forecasts are made and published. We read the reports and outlooks. But by tomorrow, we see that yesterday's forecasts are wrong. Then the process repeats itself.

If we are among those who prosper, we become skeptical about economics. We can see from firsthand experience that it doesn't work, and we develop our own methods of making forecasts that are more reliable than those we find in the news or those we can buy privately from the economic experts. But even though we become skeptical, we seldom say so. Nobody does, except an occasional journalist. It would be impolite for us to say that economics doesn't work. Economists are among the most respected of all our public figures. We may think, "Economics doesn't work, but it should. Maybe when computers are sophisticated enough, the Science of Economics will figure everything out."

But the fact remains that people in all walks of life, whether they are conducting their investments or merely following front-page developments, can have just as much insight into tomorrow's likelihoods as the best-known econometrician does—without the expensive complexity.

This should not really be surprising. A single human mind is the instrument best equipped to grasp reality in its rawest, most multidimensional form and to reason out the possibilities and probabilities. A single human mind dealing simultaneously with qualitative and quantitative analyses soundly defeats any team of technicians dealing mainly with figures.

But no matter who makes them, forecasts are almost always wrong. I have just asserted that the mind is much better than the machine, but forecasts of whatever origin are almost always wrong. This simple fact must be squarely faced. The future is an unyielding mystery. Truth with a capital "T" cannot be divined.

And yet, forecasting continues. For even if two forecasters are off by a mile, the one who is an inch closer may prosper at the other's expense. In our system of democratic capitalism, it is not necessary to foresee Truth with a capital "T," it is only necessary to more often come a little closer than your competition does.

The premise of this book is that a single human mind can beat teams of economic experts by the inch that is needed for competitive advantage, and that the winning inch can be extended—if not all the way to a mile, then by a significant amount. The ability to forecast well is not purely intuitive. It is a matter of gathering the right knowledge and applying critical thought to the facts with as much intellectual honesty as can be found. The entire process can be improved by practicing regularly, maintaining confidence in one's existing abilities, and using careful methods. The first half of this book deals with the attitudes that can enhance the ability to forecast, and the second half deals with a number of specific methods that have been found to work.

Business Without Economists is intended for anyone who must forecast. Essentially, that includes all of us. But some people depend more heavily on forecasting than others—for instance, businesspeople, commodities speculators, real estate investors, stock market participants, brokers, sales managers, fashion designers, politicians—and they would know unbounded success if they had an accurate, reliable crystal ball. Most of us would like to be able to make better forecasts, and this book requires no technical prerequisites. The challenge is one of clear thinking and reasoned judgment on matters of common knowledge to us all.

This book takes a very hard shot at professional economists. No improvement in your forecasting is possible until you explode the myth that scientific number-crunching will one day succeed and that economic computers will forecast the future. This myth has a tight hold on all of us. It represents the human quest for complete reason, with zero emotion. But as long as humans are dually rational and emotional, the best forecasting will need a dual approach.

Nothing short of a frontal assault on economics will gain us the inches we need. And yet, not all economics will be found wrong and useless. What we will do is pick and choose. If we can finally see through the overall illusion of economics as science, then, from the wreckage of the myth, we can pick the individual techniques that will strengthen our new-found attitudes about what to trust. The book is not aimed at achieving "theoretical victory," but at assisting the reader to abandon what doesn't work in favor of what does.

Chapter 1

The Demand for Gurus

Facing up to the fact that economics doesn't work and that forecasts are almost always wrong is not an enjoyable task; in fact many will find it downright threatening. For those people, it will be more comfortable to stay put, secure in the belief that all questions have answers, and that Science can supply the answers if it is allowed sufficient time and sufficient means.

Virtually nothing can be said to dispel such a belief. It might be called a core property of our culture. It is the basis of a multi-billion-dollar market for economists who say they have answers. The belief in the potential of finding "right" answers is so strong that this multi-billion-dollar market grows every day, despite the fact that right answers are rarely if ever found, and that no one is getting closer.

So it is a partnership of one person's fear of the unknowable and another person's optimism about being on the verge of scientific answers about human affairs that gives us economic gurus.

The temptation to fill this role is something I personally have felt on many occasions. In fact, the catalyst for this book was an incident at my place of work that involved the temptation to become the "Answer Man." A fellow worker, a scientist known for innovation in our research and development department, stopped me in the hall and said, "Bill, I need to talk to someone on your staff for five minutes to get some answers about the U.S. dollar."

I invited him into my office and picked up a copy of a one-page analysis that I had just finished preparing. In the wake of an announcement by the "Big Five" Finance Ministers that they were going to weaken the dollar by coordinated intervention, my one-pager gave the history of past Central Bank interventions and the lack of results against strong, underlying trends.

"Read this," I said. "It's hot off the presses and tells you everything I know." My colleague (let's call him Jim) took the paper reluctantly, thanked me, and left.

In half an hour, Jim was back. Putting the paper down on my desk, he said, "This really didn't help. Let me explain what's going on. I've been working for the last two years on a formulation that really works better than anything you can think of, and I've got one of our best customers interested in giving it a test market—but now there's a hitch. One of the chemicals is only made in Europe, and they sell it to us in foreign currency. That ingredient is a pretty big part of the cost, so I've got to know what the dollar's going to do before I can really recommend going ahead with the whole project."

A little nervously, but with complete honesty, I said, "I don't know what the dollar's going to do."

Jim looked at me blankly.

I continued: "It's not my job to know what the dollar's going to do."

Jim's brow knitted and his eyes wandered around my office—in search perhaps of a nameplate that would reassure him that he was indeed talking to the company's Director of Economic Research.

"My job is to provide you with whatever you need so that you can make up your mind *yourself* about what the dollar's going to do."

"I can't read a whole bunch of books on economics," he blustered. "I thought that was *your* job."

"You're the one who has to take the positions. I don't get paid to take those positions for you."

"I can't be responsible for the U.S. dollar," he said.

"Nobody can," I agreed. "But didn't you just tell me that you were responsible for estimating the cost of your new formula, and isn't the dollar a part of that cost?"

He leaned forward and said, "Do you or don't you think the dollar will keep getting weaker? It may cancel my project, but just give me the bottom line and I'll stop pestering you."

"Look, it's not a case of my being too busy," I said. "I'll be glad to spend as much time as you want, pull together data you believe might help, test any positions you already have, or whatever—so that you can make up your mind."

"I can't *do* that!" Jim said. "I'm not the expert on economics, *you* are!"

Seeing that we were on different wavelengths, I offered another suggestion. "Why don't you ask that one of our commodities traders be put on your development team? There are several who get paid to take positions on currency."

Jim shook his head, tossed up his arms, and started out of my office. "All I wanted was a simple answer to a simple question," he said.

In the silence of my office after Jim's departure, I contemplated the gulf between us. Jim was a professional scientist. He was expecting me, whom he regarded as another professional scientist, to share with him the fruits of my discipline. The first problem was that I did not regard economics as a scientific undertaking, and perhaps that shocked him. But more likely, what it did was to complicate his life. After two years of effort on his improved formula, he would certainly be distressed by the impingement of some "extraneous" factor, such as the dollar, and he would be in the perfect mood to wish for some magic spell to make it go away. Perhaps he wanted me to perform the magic. Then I thought, "No intelligent man living today would believe, upon careful examination, that economics is a science—especially not another scientist. The evidence of failure, the lack of results from the scientific method, is too great." But Jim was not making a careful examination; instead he was simply following a long-standing custom. In the process he was willing to accord me, on the spot, some sort of extra-rational or spiritual ability. That would solve his problem, at least in the short run. He could take my word on the path of the dollar, and put the problem out of his mind. Later, if I were wrong, and his project failed, he could point to my erroneous forecast and be absolved himself. Just now he had gotten angry because his guru-designate wouldn't play the game. On top of this, I had had the gall to suggest that predicting the basic uncertainty affecting his project was his own responsibility, not mine. How odd it must have seemed!

I then lapsed into sorrowful amusement in considering the corollary problem of how Jim's boss, and his boss's boss, could have permitted a project to go on for two years, a project that hinged so directly on the one economic variable that is the most uncertain and the least likely to forgive the frailties of economists, namely the future strength of the U.S. dollar. How many millions of dollars had we spent on the project? And how many billions of dollars were being similarly put to risk in this country, hostage not just to advancing the frontiers of chemistry (or some other legitimate science) but unwittingly to extra-rational belief in gurus?

Chapter 2

The Rise and Fall of a Soft Science

This book's assault on economics will be launched along several fronts:

1. The context of its historical development since World War II (Chapter 2).
2. The cracks now emerging in the fortress of complexity that has long protected professional economists (Chapter 3).
3. The evident differences between economic models and business reality (Chapters 4 and 5).
4. The growing disaffection of the largest customer of economics (Chapter 6).

The assault will not dislodge veteran economic professionals; such is beyond my hope. The goal instead is a short, vigorous campaign aimed at fostering new attitudes in the readers who, from their own experience, already know that economics doesn't work. Such readers are seeking greater confidence in their own abilities. They have been skeptical about economics as science all along, but have not made the irreverent leap to complete intellectual freedom. They need specific confirmation that what they believe about the weakness of economics is both rational and sound. Let us begin with a brief look at the historical context.

THE RISE

Historical treatments of economics tend not to be skeptical of its ultimate value and worth to humanity. The founders are chronicled as intellectual heroes, miraculously extracting precious concepts from a void. More recent men are described as "empirical scientists" who observe events and gather data (as if in white laboratory coats) and reach powerful new conclusions with the aid of computers.

Thus the recent history of economics is ripe for objective review. I think that the main points are as follows: First, there arose in the immediate postwar years a strong demand for economic advice, especially from government—emanating from the "can do," central-planning approaches that were seen as having won the war. The amount of government-generated economic data increased, and an adequate supply of researchers emerged to meet the demand for answers, ever ready (as any of us are) for fortune, fame, and honor. "Experts" cropped up all over the country, many of them scientists in disciplines that are today called the "hard" sciences (for example, physics, chemistry, mathematics). Practitioners of the new "soft" sciences, including social science, political science, and economics, sought the same status as other experts. The transference of quantitative methods to the soft sciences was fascinating, and those bureaucrats already disposed to believe in central planning (as opposed to the "invisible hand") were intrigued. Maybe the day of rational control over man's affairs was dawning. And the 1950s and 1960s provided the new economists with a nearly ideal period for successful forecasting: The country was at peace, it was as yet relatively unregulated (though the economists would themselves help to change that), and, above all, it was isolated from foreign economies by an effective monetary agreement (the 1946 Bretton Woods agreement, which established fixed exchange rates) and by nearly absolute military hegemony. Terrorism was a local, not international, phenomenon, and Islamic rulers sat atop their oil reserves placidly accepting a mere $1.80 per barrel, year after year. Businesses began employing economists in great numbers in order to better coordinate their inventory levels with cycles in the economy. Economists began increasingly to argue about goals with other economists in the government and to explain conditions for or against their profits to stockholders and the public.

Just as the regime of the 1950s and 1960s was about to break down and the internationalization of the U.S. economy was beginning, computer technology arrived on the scene (this was not coincidental) and promised economists a new lease on life. The application of statistical methods to economic data via large computer models, employing initially dozens and later hundreds and even thousands of simultaneous equations, was called "econometrics." The debut of this new method, or certainly the most important single instance, occurred in 1972 when work done at MIT was published by The Club of Rome; it was called *The Limits to Growth*. This book provided the public with its first wide exposure to the techniques of computer modelling, and the mere fact that the models were done on computers seemed to lend inordinate credibility to the book's thesis. The thesis was not new; it dates from Malthus or before, and had in fact been re-detailed in the early 1960s by the novelist Saul Bellow in *Mr. Sammler's Planet*—a signal from the arts that the time was right for the idea. The public infatuation with *Limits* and its computerized analyses was immense. And at just this time, the rulers of Islam turned implacid and attacked the western world via OPEC. Prices of oil skyrocketed, and *The Limits to Growth* seemed prophetic.

FOUNDATION FOR THE FALL

At about the same time as OPEC's initial price attack on the West, the Bretton Woods monetary agreement was abrogated.

Not only did oil prices rise, but so did the price of gold, other precious metals, commodities, and all raw materials. Exchange rates began a new era of volatility.

The demand for oil, even at quadrupled prices, continued to increase and many countries borrowed money to pay for it. The increased oil revenues went first to OPEC countries and then to their international banks, which recycled the funds back to the oil users. A global capital market emerged, generally referred to as Eurocredit. More Eurodollars were created than the total of all domestic U.S. dollars. This "off-shore" money is outside the control of the U.S. Federal Reserve Bank, but it is nonetheless real. It can be borrowed; it pays bills. Over $2 trillion in Euromoney has been created, and annual interbank trading in Euromoney rose to $75 *trillion* in the mid-1980s. This is about 25 times greater than the funds needed for world trade of all goods. In addition, foreign exchange trading rose to about $35 trillion per year in the same period, about 12 times greater than actual, physical trade.

Business author Peter F. Drucker, writing in the Spring 1986 issue of *Foreign Affairs,* calls this emergence of global capital markets a "symbol" economy, as opposed to the "real" economy. He says, "Economists assume that the 'real' economy and 'symbol' economy will come together again." But this needn't happen.

> These changes are permanent rather than cyclical. We may never understand what caused them—the causes of economic change are rarely simple. It may be a long time before economic theorists accept that there have been fundamental changes, and longer still before they adapt their theories to account for them. Above all, they will surely be most reluctant to accept that it is the world economy in control, rather than the macroeconomics of the nation-state on which most economic theory still exclusively focuses.[1]

Business Week calls today's foreign exchange markets "casinos." Foreign exchange takes place in trader-to-trader speculation, in the same manner as commodities futures markets, although as yet mainly without designated pits and formal rules of the game. These exchange markets provide rational ways for participants to lay off risks in a very uncertain world. But such markets are notoriously unsuited to economic analysis based on the common sense of supply-and-demand scenarios. The markets are only "rational" because they permit "emotional" participants (speculators) to enter into the action. Thus the newest, most global markets of our day, the financials, are dually rational and emotional—to an extent that few professional bankers or bank economists will ever admit. As we head into a greater and greater emergence of global financial casinos, forecasting—especially that based on scientific models—becomes less and less reliable.

In the past few years there have been many articles explicitly challenging the myth that economics works. For example, headlines like "Economists Are This Year's Endangered Species," "Economists Missing the Mark; More Tools, Bigger Errors," "Maybe Economists Should Be a Little Less Positive," and "Oil Prices: Living with the Perils of Prophecy" all appeared in major newspapers and magazines in late 1984 or early 1985. There have also been quite a few scholarly articles on the subject, dealing mainly with the fact that forecasts are rarely correct; for example, "Are Economic Forecasters Worth Listening To?" (*Harvard Business Review*, Sept.–Oct., 1984), "The Track Record of Macroeconomic Forecasts" (*New England Economic Review*, Nov.–Dec., 1983), and "The Accuracy of Individual and Group Forecasts from Business Outlook Surveys" (National Bureau of Standards, *Working Paper*, 1982).

Business, however, remains deeply committed to economics. According to a study by *Petroleum Intelligence Weekly*, "On the order of half a trillion dollars was invested around the world in 1980–81 alone—on the mistaken assumption that oil prices would rise steadily for the rest of this century."[2] Indeed, as I write this in the summer of 1986, the Third World debt explosion that was associated with the oil boom and bust is now over $1 trillion. Economists are still pursuing econometrics and business is still buying the forecasts—as though the largest, most potentially threatening debt in the history of mankind has nothing to do with the myth of economics as science.

Drucker says, "Practitioners, whether in government or in business, cannot wait until there is a new theory. They have to act. And their actions will be more likely to succeed the more they are based on the new realities of a changed world economy."[3]

I would add that their actions will also be more likely to succeed the more they are based on what works, rather than what doesn't. History shows that economic forecasts don't work, and suggests that they will get worse rather than better.

Chapter 3

Economic Complexity and Circularity

What most protects economics from attack is its complexity. But what defeats it most surely, in the minds of those who try to apply its results to the marketplace, is its circularity.

Complexity works as a defense of economics in the following way: If you approach a professional economist, especially an econometrician, with a desire to understand his arguments by casting them in plain language, he will say that such a method will oversimplify things, and that his proposition must use mathematics, often rather advanced mathematics. He may call your desire for plain language a case of *"Wall Street Journal* economics" that doesn't merit serious attention. If you want to persevere in your desire to understand him, then you must take up the study of mathematics.

When you are finally facile enough with figures and formulas to come once again into his economic theories, you will find that, yes, there have been no violations of mathematical principles. The algebraic conclusions will be well correlated with the input data. In other words, within the context of scientific analysis, the economist is scientific. If this satisfies you, you become a disciple. What you are then advocating is that science, in its full rigor and strictness, captures human affairs.

The process by which a serious student penetrates the complexity and then becomes an advocate of economics is self-serving, for at some point every such student must admit that the principles apply to ideal markets, not to real ones. If you accept such an abstraction, you become a believer. This builds in a fail-safe condition: Within ideal markets, the principles of economics operate in mathematical precision; when principles fail to fore-cast results in actual markets, it is not the fault of the Science of Economics, but the fault of the markets for not being ideal. Something is interfering with the way the markets *should* work. Such interferences are labelled "artificial." To those who must operate in such markets, however, the interferences are much more real than artificial. Participants in real markets wish that someone would help explain artificial irregularities rather than mathematicize what the regularities *would* be if they were free to be ideal.

Thus the present chapter will not attempt to penetrate, in mathematical terms, the complexity of economics, and show it to be unsound. Instead we will sample the complexity in its plain-language form, attempting to appreciate how the desire for greater and greater reason lures us into the trap of mathematical formulation. We will then take a tour of Economic Circularity, and we'll attempt to spring the trap of pure logic in order to liberate critical thinking.

A SAMPLE OF COMPLEXITY

Suppose we recall my colleague, Jim, and his frustration with the U.S. dollar. How would an economist explain the changes in the exchange value of the dollar?

The traditional theory on exchange rates, still widely held in Europe, is based on the relative changes between countries in the prices of goods—that is, the relative changes in rates of inflation.

Almost immediately, complexity is upon us, because the concept of "inflation" is surrounded by fog. The novice must concentrate hard on the special language of economics, putting in the place of the word "inflation" the phrase "rising prices." The novice must form a mental image of rising prices by picturing the rising line of a graph.

Consider two countries, A and B, which each produce shoes:

	A	B
Price of shoes, each	$1.00	£1.00

If the shoes are identical in all respects, and if the same is true of all other goods, then the exchange rate should be one-to-one:

$$\$1.00 = £1.00$$

Now let's say that Country B, over a period of time, suffers from inflation; that is, the price of its shoes goes up:

	A	B
Month 1	$1.00	£1.00
Month 2	1.00	1.50
Month 3	1.00	2.00

All potential buyers of shoes would look with disfavor on Country B. B's price has risen too high. Buyers will not travel to Country B, and there will be little traffic at its borders and few people in its exchange office wanting its currency. The value of its currency will fall—due to the inflation in B's prices. Soon we might see a posting at the exchange window:

$$\$1.00 = £2.00$$

This says that one dollar will get you two pounds, which in turn will buy one pair of shoes (in Country B).

The generalized form of this theory is: "The higher a country's rate of inflation, the lower its currency's exchange value." Complexity again. Many readers can follow the simple example above, but may have trouble with the general "law." The trouble sets in when the shift is made from plain language to formal language. A formal language is the same as a foreign language, except that the letters and spelling of the words don't change, only their meanings.

To learn foreign languages takes practice. To learn economics requires going over and over examples such as the above on A's and B's shoes, until the generality about inflation causing lower exchange rates becomes "grooved."

Suppose you take the time to do this. What next? More complexity.

The first problem is that pairs of shoes are rarely identical. It is hard even to imagine that two pairs of shoes, one from England and the other from Italy, would be *similar*, let alone identical.

The second problem is that, within any given country, the price of "shoes," as a general product category, is rarely known. The government may sample a few brands, but not all, and not all models within a brand. The government's sample of shoe prices, identified perhaps as Standard Industrial Category (SIC) 314, might be gathered and published—not in time to guide today's shoe buyer, but with a delay of many months. Actual buyers will make up their minds on their *own* sample of prices, including those that might be classed as "special offers" or "volume purchases."

The third problem, or course, is that "shoes" is but one category of the millions of categories of products that make up a modern economy. Each and every category defies easy definition; at some point, with a bit of additional leather, shoes become boots. What the government statistician does is to sample a broad range of products, sometimes called a *market basket* and compare this with the same sample of goods at an earlier time. But goods change over time. A pair of shoes today does not look like a pair from 1950 or 1960. The style and the quality have changed. The intangibles associated with the cost to manufacture the shoes have changed—that is, there may be new safety regulations today, regarding arch supports or other aspects. Certain kinds of jogging shoes common today did not even exist a decade ago. How can jogging shoes be added to the market basket of 1986 shoe prices?

One item that might at first seem more stable and common across both time and nationality is money itself. After all, money is money, right? Suppose the item under consideration for purchase is money itself, which is desirable for its earning power (interest rate) in its native country. Let's say that the prime rate in Country A is 10 percent compared with 7 percent in Country B. Wouldn't this mean that buyers seeking a 10 percent return instead of a 7 percent one would begin lining up at A's exchange office? And that A would then hold out for a greater rate of exchange?

But other problems arise at this point: Country A may have a low rate of inflation on its goods compared with the rate in other countries, which should strengthen its currency—but it may be paying a low prime rate of interest, which should have the opposite effect of weakening its currency. How do you combine these two forces to get at the aggregate effect on exchange rates, especially in the real world, which produces millions of different types of goods? Also, Country A may have more than one price for its money—it may have prime rate (which sometimes varies from city to city or from day to day); it may have 30-, 90-, and 180-day T-bills with different rates; it may have stock markets and money markets that offer (or promise to offer) different rates; and so on. Furthermore, Country A may have regulations on how much a foreigner will be taxed on earnings from owning A's currency, before the foreigner can take the interest payments home to Country B. And of course the investor or trader from Country B may have to face other such regulations at home.

The economist approaching this complexity must approach it with two theories: One for how economies work, and a second for how to sample an economy to see if the first theory is correct.

Economists often lament, "There's not enough data," or "The data is not good enough." This will always be the cry. Measurement will never catch up with unfolding reality. As Drucker says, "Practitioners cannot wait until there is a new theory. They have to act."[1] Actions are dually rational and emotional. No amount of rational complexity will forecast dual actions.

Complexity is less a fortress to be revered than a delusion to be discarded.

A SAMPLE OF CIRCULARITY

The rise in value of the U.S. dollar in the 1980s was a surprise to most people, especially in its duration and magnitude. As is always the case, there were several schools of thought on how this had come about. The two most dominant theories were as follows:

Theory A: Deficit Starts Everything

1. Federal government runs fiscal deficit.
2. Therefore, government has to borrow more money than normal.
3. Therefore, borrowers are crowded out of the common pool of savings and credit (money supply), which is being kept tight by the Fed (which means low inflation).
4. Therefore, interest rates increase.
5. Therefore, the dollar is strong.
6. Therefore, a trade deficit develops.
7. Therefore, merchandise payments flow out of the country.
8. Therefore, foreigners have money to invest back in the United States to earn high interest rates.
9. Therefore, capital investment flows into our country from abroad, in essence serving to finance our government deficit.

Theory B: Capital Flows Come First School

1. The United States is an attractive place for investment, due to high economic growth, high profits, low taxes, high political stability.
2. Therefore, capital investment flows into our country.
3. Therefore, the dollar is strong.
4. Therefore, foreign goods are cheap.
5. Therefore, a trade deficit develops (if foreign goods are of sufficient quality to be desired.)
6. Separately, heavy defense spending is required to keep our country safe and stable.
7. Therefore, a federal budget deficit exists, unless Congress cuts spending in other areas.

Both of these models are familiar and we have all heard the arguments in favor of and against them. Both of them "make sense," but they differ in what can be called the direction of causality. In other words, each model is a circle of logical elements. In Theory A you start at one point and travel in one direction. In Theory B you start at another point and travel in another direction. Many of the points of the arguments are the same, you just approach them up one street instead of another.

Theory A and Theory B about the dollar are examples of *economic circularity*. The person listening to the theories doesn't know which one is correct. A good speaker, whether economist or politician, can make either one sound right. An economist does this by saying that the data make it so; a politician does it by intonation and moral appeal. For many years now, listeners, who have gotten generally skeptical of politicians, have been taking economists at their word—that the data bear out the arguments. But this too is happening less often, as it dawns on listeners that the economists are no more right about the future than politicians are.

Economic circularity is caused by the fact that data have no direction. Data are points. Connections between points must be made by those who use the data. Data do not, in and of themselves, demand to be connected in one and only one direction.

To believe that economists work over the data on the economy in the same way that chemists work out the formula for a new compound is a serious flaw in critical thinking. Chemists have two advantages: (1) They can connect the data in any way they like and then test their theory against reality and (2) If they have insufficient data to complete a theory, they can measure the compound anew, from as many different ways as they like. Economists can test theories only against other theories. "History" itself is, after all, only a theory, subject to vast differences in interpretation. Economists cannot go back to the lab and make more measurements; they are stuck, let's say in the case of U.S. GNP, with what the government publishes (first as a "prelim," then as a "revised," then as a "final," and then—after a few months or years—as another "revised").

ABANDON DATA, ABANDON SCIENCE?

The reader might at this point begin to wonder if this book is on its way to recommending the complete abandonment of data and of scientific method.

Such a reader might ask, "You wouldn't say that we should close our eyes to the data, would you? Isn't it better to go as far as possible with scientific methods, before backing off to a compromise position? Don't most economists compromise? They're not all *purists*, are they?"

It is true that many if not most economists compromise—but I would say that they are forced to against their will. The goal of the discipline is to push science, to the exclusion of all else, as far as it will possibly go—in the hope (and belief) that it will one day go all the way. My view is that this doesn't work, and that a scientific approach to economic forecasting must be challenged before the reader can assume the most useful new attitudes. The need for balance must be recognized *before*, not after, science fails.

Chapter 4

Economic Models versus Reality

Recognizing that an economic theory (or model) is different from reality is crucial. We may say that we know this very well. But put us in front of a well-spoken economist who is armed with pages of data, computer printouts, and graphs and we will very likely become mesmerized. We are conditioned to believe that someone, somewhere, knows how the facts of the economy all fit together, or that someone should. In short, we *want* to believe that the economy can be successfully modelled, mathematically, like a smooth-running top. We want to believe it so badly, apparently, that we overlook a decade of failed economic models and we keep on buying new ones.

Is bad information better than no information at all? Psychologists would no doubt say that this apparent need to be comforted about the future is a central feature of the relationship between the businessperson and the economist; without introducing psychology, it is nearly impossible to explain the extent to which both have ignored reality.

But let us return to the quicksand at the philosophical heart of economics and sink in a little further, before stepping out onto more solid ground—which will be our goal in the second half of this book. It may be that readers are not yet fully convinced of what I assert about economic circularity and the fact that both businesspeople and economists tend to confuse economic models with reality. Once again, it will not be possible to *prove* this assertion, but it may be helpful to develop it more fully.

The principal differences between economic models and reality are summarized in Figure 4–1, which I recommend that the reader study before going on.

Difference A: In Economic Models, Facts Are Facts.
In Reality, Facts Are Slippery. Everything Depends on Your Point of View and the Context.

Most of us have had the real-life experience of witnessing an event as fact, and then learning that other observers give quite a different account of the event, according to their point of view and the context of explanation.

To further develop this thesis that "facts are slippery," let's continue with the general issue of the dollar and trade. Speaking in October of 1985, Representative Richard A. Gephardt of Missouri told a reporter doing a story on the movement toward protectionism in Congress, "Trade is the one place where we have a tangible symptom of the Republican-Reagan fiscal policy. *The trade deficit is a fact. People can see it and understand it.*"

When I first read this statement, my mind began picturing ships at the dock with crowds of people standing around, perhaps trying to count the Toyotas and Audis as they came ashore, maybe putting their hands on each one to make the arrival tangible, and then, when the count reached 100 vehicles, I imagined that a pink slip would arrive for one of the bystanders notifying him that he was no longer needed at the Ford plant where he worked.

The facts of trade are by no means certain, let alone the facts of the trade deficit. It is by no means certain that every ship arriving at every port is *counted,* its cargo registered in government logs, the data entered into a computer, the computer tapes sent to a regional accounting center, the contents of 100 tapes summed by 1,000 merchandise categories (each requiring judgment), the aggregates sent to Washington on other tapes, and so

Figure 4-1. Differences between economic models and economic reality.

In Economic Models	*In Reality*
A. Facts are facts.	Facts are slippery. Everything depends on your point of view and the context.
B. Government indicators are discrete and solid.	Government indicators are based on sampling. They are aggregates or averages that require judgment by their authors, and they are subject not only to revision but to redefinition to suit political goals.
C. Data is available for every variable; events can be quantified; statistical discrepancies can be ignored.	Events defy quantification; important factors cannot be measured at all, let alone with precision.
D. Equilibrium is assumed to exist; from this base things cycle.	The universe is not obliged to be in any given condition, let alone in equilibrium.
E. There are both dependent and independent variables.	There are no independent variables.
F. Going from tons of indicators and equations to hundreds or to thousands is good, and will improve the reliability of forecasts.	Sheer size of models will not convert data to reality, especially as long as the universe contains free will.
G. "The Economy" exists, as an aggregate entity.	"The Economy" doesn't exist. There are 230 million separate people, each with their own goals, falling into various groupings (subsectors or special interests).

forth, until a monthly import and a monthly export figure are arrived at and published (as "preliminary").

At best, existing government data give only a rough idea of what the magnitudes may be in the flows of merchandise. The data of themselves do not say why the merchandise was bought, or who the final consumer will be, or especially whether there are connections to other aspects of social life. Gephardt's connection between these data points and the "Republican-Reagan fiscal policy" seems to me far from "tangible." What Gephardt's statements really mean, I think, is this: "People believe me when I tell them that the trade deficit is a fact, that it's hurting them, and that it's the fault of Reagan and the Republicans." Gephardt receives the published figures on exports and imports from the Department of Commerce and then links them (in the way he wants) to other data he's aware of—for the data in their raw form are simply not connected. There are no crowds at the ports being diminished by pink slips as a result of the foreign vessels, there are only longshoremen, who run the cranes, and inspectors, who make a few sample checks between physical inventory and bills of lading and then send a new form on its way to the computer.

At this point, the reader may say, "You're nitpicking. We all *know* there's a trade deficit." I say that what we know is that there's a trade deficit being reported. That much is clear, and that much only. The reports contain the trade deficit's approximate magnitude, according to the abilities, judgment, and sampling methods of government officials. The reports do not contain, inherently, the reasons for a trade deficit. Reasons require the interpreter of data to make connections with other data, which themselves are no more certain than the type we've just discussed. If the report of the trade deficit is seen in a newspaper, it will be accompanied by a headline, chosen by an editor with his or her own views on how to connect things, and it will also be accompanied by the interpretations of big-name economists, who believe they know connections better than we, and perhaps by political dogma, as in the case mentioned above.

In the same interview, Senator Lloyd Bentsen of Texas agreed with Gephardt. Bentsen said, "As you see more and more erosion of jobs, you see more and more families relating to this issue [trade]. All theories are swept aside. They're talking about the realities." Bentsen's argument is that two series of data are connected: The approximate magnitude of the merchandise trade deficit and the approximate magnitude of unemployment. In fact, Bentsen is making an even more precise connection than that, for the reports on employment showed that the United States gained, not lost, about 4 million jobs in a four-year period (1981–1985) during which the trade balance swung from positive to negative. The Senator is apparently connecting the trade deficit to just one aspect of employment, namely manufacturing, which reportedly has gone down by 750,000 jobs in the period. So while more people are indeed at work, Bentsen implies that they are at work in jobs inferior to the 1 million manufacturing jobs no longer reported.

However, we do not have data on the pay levels of either the 4 million new jobs or the 1 million old manufacturing jobs. Maybe most of the displaced manufacturing workers got the higher paying service jobs. "No way," a politician might say at this point; "I don't need the precise data, all I need is the direct contact of my constituents." In which event, I rest my case about his brand of economics not being scientific.

Difference B: In Economic Models, Government Indicators Are Discrete and Solid.
In Reality, Government Indicators Are Based on Sampling. They Are Aggregates or Averages that Require Theories and Judgment by Their Authors, and They Are Subject not Only to Revision but to Redefinition to Suit Political Goals.

Senator Bentsen is well aware of the next item in Figure 4-1, that government indicators are by no means solid and concrete. In September of 1984, Senator Bentsen accused the Administration of cooking the numbers. According to a report in *The New York Times*, Bentsen made the complaint after the Department of Commerce released its "flash" estimate of the third quarter 1984 gross national product (GNP), which it said was 3.6 percent, and which Bentsen argued was only 2.2 percent. The difference is in how the Department of Commerce should treat the fact that three General Motors plants, which produce about 7 percent of the nation's cars, were closed for extensive retooling during the second quarter. The Senator argued that Commerce normally takes this into account in second quarter GNP, but that since the second quarter GNP was a rosy 7.1 percent, government economists postponed the 1.4 percent boost in the estimate to the third quarter. According to *The Times,* Commerce officials passed the controversy up the line of management, and so far as I know today, there was no change in the original judgment made. The third quarter GNP was indeed revised, as is always the case, as we went from "flash," to "prelim," to "revised," to "final," and so on, but the outside observer has no way of knowing what decisions were made, against what criteria, in the bowels of Commerce.

The above example involving General Motors plants is not a case of one party being "right" and the other "wrong," or vice versa. It is simply an illustration of the ever present force of qualitative judgment in an area popularly mistaken to be purely quantitative and scientific. Politicians don't mind having it both ways. It was Bentsen in 1984 saying that the data had been cooked, and it was Bentsen in 1985 saying that the data proved his case: "All theories are swept aside. They're talking about realities."

Allow me one further example of the process of data revision and the softness of government data. On July 21, 1984, a headline in the business section of *The New York Times* read, "U.S., Revising GNP of 1977, Adds 3% Growth." According to the story, the 1977 GNP was being changed from 5.5 percent to 8.5 percent. "Most of the additional $58.2 billion in economic activity, the Department of Commerce said, was accounted for by $47.6 billion of 'improved adjustments for misreporting on tax returns' of small proprietors, and by estimates for people who filed no tax returns." A Commerce official commented, "Most misreporting clearly stems from the desire of the taxpayer to evade taxes."[1]

Here we encounter a terrible reality for would-be econometric modellers:

1. Society is not made up of citizens and businesses eagerly trying to cooperate with government data collection—in fact, just the opposite situation exists. Many if not most citizens are at all times assiduously hiding data. The so-called "underground" economy is apparently enormous, in the tens or hundreds of billions of dollars (especially when drugs, prostitution, and organized crime are added).

2. Government is willing and able to change annual data by significant amounts, and will do so many years after the data were thought to be final. As the Commerce Department "improves" its methods of inferring tax evasion, it will gradually revise the GNPs for years subsequent to 1977.

What really did happen in 1977? Should we believe that the level of economic activity was 5.5 percent, or was it really 8.5 percent? Should we change all our historical models, or should we assume that business and markets reacted to the contemporary reports, and had no sure knowledge that the underground was doing this much or that much? In fact, do markets only react to "prelims", and not to subsequent "revisions" or "finals?" Or do markets, in their essence, *know* the true, underlying conditions more accurately than any government will ever report them?

Difference C: In Economic Models, Data Are Available for Every Variable; Events Can Be Quantified; Statistical Discrepancies Can Be Ignored.
In Reality, Events Defy Quantification; Important Factors Cannot Be Measured at All, Let Alone with Precision.

In international economics, how do you treat countries in which there is no department of commerce, or in which such function is not as sophisticated as ours? And what about countries in which there is not only tax evasion, but civil war?

I have argued above that government data are approximations, and I want to point out now that no one knows this any better than those who collect the data; such people go to considerable lengths to point out discrepancies to would-be users.

As an example, let's continue with the issue of trade, and consider a data series published each quarter by the Department of Commerce (in *Survey of Current Business*) called "U.S. International Transactions." In a single table, Commerce gives its data for the so-called "current account" of the United States, and the "capital account." The table is very similar in concept to a typical family budget. For instance, in a family budget there is current income and expenses, as well as assets and debt. Suppose your income is relatively fixed (as is the income from this country's exports of goods). Now suppose that your expenses go up, perhaps even dramatically (as has the expense of this country's import of foreign goods). If your monthly expenses are greater than your monthly income, it is said by economists that your current account is in deficit. You must either sell off a piece of property, or you must borrow. In other words, a deficit in your current account must be exactly balanced by some change in your *capital account*. If not, you face such serious unpleasantries as criminal prosecution or bankruptcy.

At the national level, the current account is what's popularly called the "trade balance;" it is the sum of exports minus imports. The capital account is the sum of increases or decreases in assets, held either by foreigners in the United States or by American citizens in foreign countries. In other words, the current account is the balance of what we're spending in the short term to purchase goods and services for immediate consumption; the capital account is the balance of how much we have invested in assets overseas versus how much foreigners own in investments here. Debts or loans are regarded as assets (to the lender), and fall into the capital account.

Common sense tells us that the data in the U.S. International Transactions Table should "add up;" that is, if there is a deficit in trade, then we've paid out money to buy things, and such money must show up as an *asset* in some foreigner's account—whether it's simply held as a cash deposit or is invested back in some dollar-denominated instrument.

Following are data from two columns of Commerce's U.S. International Transactions Table, taken over a ten-year period (figures represent billions of dollars):

Year	Current Account	Capital Account	Statistical Discrepancy
1975	$18.1	− $24.0	$5.9
1976	4.2	− 14.8	10.5
1977	− 14.5	16.5	− 2.0
1978	− 15.4	2.9	12.5
1979	− 1.0	− 24.4	25.4
1980	1.9	− 26.9	25.0
1981	6.3	− 26.6	20.3
1982	− 8.1	− 24.8	32.8
1983	− 40.8	29.3	11.5
1984	− 101.5	76.9	24.7

It is apparent that the current account and the capital account columns don't match up. The discrepancy should be "zero" in each year, but instead the discrepancy is often quite large. The discrepancy is also called "errors and omissions." In 1982, for instance, the errors and omissions were $32.8 billion, which was four times greater than the current account (the trade deficit).

Government statisticians clearly label the limits of this data, but users are not deterred. "This is the best idea we've got," they may say. Or, "There *is* no other data." I disagree. Why must we be compelled to use bad data, and to believe that it will lead to useful forecasts?

Some readers may be saying to themselves, "I don't believe this guy! Where's he getting his information? He must be cooking the data just like the politicians do." If those readers are motivated to go to their libraries, find the latest issue of *Survey of*

Current Business, which has the U.S. International Transactions Table, spend a few minutes studying the accounting categories and checking the arithmetic, and then perhaps telephoning an analyst at the Department of Commerce and asking for an explanation of "statistical discrepancy"—then one of the main goals of this book will have been served. The careful examination of government data for the method (theory) of its collection and the limits of its accuracy leads to much more genuine and useful knowledge, in my view, than the econometric number-crunching that dominates the research scene today.

The usual assumption about the statistical discrepancy in the U.S. International Transactions Table is that it implies the existence of *unrecorded* capital flows, perhaps short-term investment instruments. I agree that this sounds logical, but my job here is to separate models from reality: No one knows what the statistical discrepancy is. No one, nowhere.

Outside the United States, data become more and more inaccurate. For example, here is the statistical discrepancy in the world current account, as kept by the International Monetary Fund (again, figures shown represent billions of dollars):

Year	Payments Balance (Errors and Omissions) of World Current Account
1977	$-9.5
1978	-7.8
1979	-7.6
1980	-19.1
1981	-56.0
1982	-95.8
1983	-63.5
1984	-71.4
1985	-88.3

How is it that payments made for the trade of goods and services in and out of all the world's countries don't add up, and are often off by amounts that are larger than the entire trade deficit of the United States? My answer: The world is not obliged to add up. The world is what it is. It is only us, with our economic models, who think things should add up. Reality is free to be reality.

Difference D: In Economic Models, Equilibrium Is Assumed to Exist; from This Base Things Cycle.
In Reality, The Universe Is Not Obliged to Be in Any Given Condition, Let Alone in Equilibrium.

The previous line of thought takes us naturally to Item D of Figure 4-1, which concerns equilibrium. I contend that, in reality, the affairs of man don't necessarily have to be in equilibrium, whereas economic models always assume that the affairs of man vary from a norm of stability, usually in cyclical fashion. The assumption of equilibrium is almost synonymous with modelling, because mathematics itself, until very recently, dealt only with phenomena that were smooth and continuous.

Human affairs, however, do not run smoothly. Events are singular and can change economics. For example: President Reagan sends Navy planes to intercept an Egyptian airliner carrying terrorists who hijacked an Italian cruise ship and killed an American tourist; the Italian government collapses over its handling of the event. Will the next government institute new economic policies? The Egyptian government complains bitterly; as the largest customer of U.S. wheat flour, will it now limit trade with the United States and go elsewhere for its bread? Will this affect our GNP? Discontinuous events, such as wars, famines, embargos, and unforeseen calamities, take place frequently. How can we make use of formulas which don't take these unknowns into account? In the last decade or so, a new branch of mathematics, called catastrophe theory, has emerged as a candidate for systematically handling discontinuity, but I have yet to see it applied to economic modelling.

The concept of equilibrium in economic modelling is flawed in yet another very important way concerning the nature of credit and money. In a barter society everything should tote up; it is possible to imagine that each and every good is inventoried in preparation for bartering against what the population may want; if you want something and don't have something else to barter for it, you'll have to do without. "I'd promise to pay later," you may say. But your promise, if accepted, would create *credit*.

Once you leave the barter system for a system of money and credit, why should you expect equilibrium? You will never have enough money at hand to buy the goods you want at the prices they carry, and the natural tendency will be to create money and credit faster than the pace at which the production of goods is proceeding. In this light, then, it should come as no big surprise that no one, nowhere, has a table that adds up the world capital account. If someone, somewhere, did, the statistical discrepancy would be very large. The creation of credit, worldwide, is not under control, a situation attested to by the dramatic emergence lately of Third World debt; indeed, inasmuch as there is no "world government" today, we should not have been expecting equilibrium in world capital flows, even to the rather sloppy accuracies obtained in the United States.

*Difference E: In Economic Models, There Are Both Dependent and
Independent Variables.
In Reality, There Are No Independent Variables.*

The chief economist of Saloman Brothers of New York is Henry Kaufman, a man often referred to in news stories as a "guru" or "high priest of economics." In testimony before Congress on June 5, 1985, Mr. Kaufman zeroed in on the difficulty of defining "money," as attempted by the U.S. Federal Reserve Bank. He said that questions should be raised "about the validity of targeting some narrowly defined concept of money as a way of influencing the behavior of the economy," because "increased versatility of credit card usage, computer access by many to funds transfers, and virtually instant investment allocations" make "money" too hard to define.[2] In other words, credit is created independent of government control.

In Kaufman's testimony, we have an example of what George Orwell, in *1984,* called "double-think": One of the most famous of all gurus says that money can't be precisely defined, but no one believes him. Instead, he is taken to mean that we've got to try harder, tighten our measurements, refine our equations, and increase the complexity of our models. In the end, more expensive computers are requisitioned and purchased.

In an equation of the form

$$y = x_1 \times x_2$$

y is considered to be a dependent variable, and x_1 and x_2 are independent variables. In other words, *y* is what you want to predict, and *y* depends on x_1 and x_2. Both of the *x* terms are assumed to exist independently of each other and of *y*.

Let us now look at an equation for GNP of the same form:

$$GNP = M_1 \times V_6$$

where M_1 = money supply
V = velocity of money

What this equation says is that the gross national product can be defined as the supply of money multiplied by the number of times that this supply is spent each year. If the supply of money increases and velocity doesn't change, then GNP can grow. If the supply of money decreases, then GNP will go down, unless the velocity at which people spend money increases.

As an ideal statement, there's nothing wrong with the GNP equation. It ought to work that way. Unfortunately, as we know from Kaufman (and from our own experience of receiving unsolicited Mastercards in the mail), money won't hold still to be quantified as needed in the equation. Furthermore, it turns out that velocity won't hold still either, in fact much less so than money supply. There is, in fact, no way to *measure* velocity; it can be *calculated* by dividing GNP by M_1, after you think you have good measurements of both GNP and M_1. If velocity is made the dependent variable, and the *price* of money, namely the interest rate, is made the independent variable, then velocity appears to change with the magnitude of interest rates. The usual interpretation is that if rates are low, people tend to be more active in spending whatever supply of money is out there. If rates are high, people's confidence goes down, and they hold back a little on velocity. The annual turnover of the supply of money goes down.

But if this is so, does GNP really decrease? After all, isn't GNP more *real* than a hypothetical product of money and its velocity? Can't we express GNP in terms of things more physical?

The equation

$$GNP = units \times price$$

may at first look more "real" than the previous one with money supply and velocity, until we recall that we cannot measure what the equation requires as inputs. We cannot measure how many units were sold in the economy nor the specific price involved in each transaction. Picture your favorite ice cream stand; does the proprietor report the number of cones sold and the price of each? Or does he report his gross sales in dollars, less his costs? And doesn't he "inflate" the costs to decrease his taxes?

There are virtually innumerable ways of expressing GNP in equation form. Another popular one among those worried by the trade deficit is

$$GNP = GND - imports,$$

where GND = gross national demand

Now the equation has a "supply side" and a "demand side." The argument is that part of the national demand that would have been served by national production (and thus jobs) is siphoned off to imports.

Each of the formulas used in modelling the economy demonstrates economic circularity. An econometric model is a set of such circularities in overlapping array. When this is perceived, the surprise diminishes that the models are never right. A key difference between economic models and reality is that the latter is not obliged to provide "independent" variables; reality is heavily interconnected, and in any ways it wants to be.

Difference F: In Economic Models, Going from Tens of Indicators and Equations to Hundreds or to Thousands Is Good, and Will Improve the Reliability of Forecasts.

In Reality, Sheer Size of Models Will Not Convert Data to Reality, Especially as Long as the Universe Contains Free Will.

The dedicated econometrician reading this will scoff. (However, I think we can safely assume that there won't be any dedicated econometricians reading this.) Rather than engage me at the philosophical level, the econometrician will reverently return to his computer and continue the battle. He will add a few dozen more equations to his network. He will include new data and revisions of old data that had been revised earlier. He will structure his assumptions more carefully and more elaborately (without of course noticing that the biggest assumption of all, equilibrium, remains firmly at the base of his work). And at some point he will make new pronouncements. They will be wrong, as they have been in the past, but it won't matter. The news media will be drawn to them, out of custom, or perhaps to report that a million dollars was spent on the effort or that more thousands of equations than ever have now been crunched. And for a short period, until events undo him, the econometrician's forecast will become a benchmark—in the news, among government officials, and even among business people.

I once took a guided tour of a major econometric firm and its computer facilities; there were literally acres of mainframes. Dozens of engineers were on duty at all times to keep the machines running, and to continue expanding the capacity. A separate electrical power supply was provided, to keep the machines up in the event of failure by the public utility. The forecast from such a multi-acre econometric model seems to stand up from a crowd of mere human beings and say, "Look, I

did calculations you can never hope to do, and until you get
smarter, fellows, you'd better pay attention to me. The world is
getting more and more complicated, and your only hope is to use
me—forget your puny common sense!"

*Difference G: In Economic Models, "The Economy" Exists, as an
Aggregate Entity.
In Reality, "The Economy" Doesn't Exist. There Are 230 Million
Separate People, Each with Their Own Goals, Falling into Various
Groupings (Subsectors or Special Interests).*

There is no such thing, in reality, as The American Economy, with capital letters. The United States is made up of a
network of competing economies, some of which sometimes
prosper at the expense of others in the same network. These
competing economies are connected, some more and some less,
with other competing economies abroad. Even within a single
competing economy in the U.S. network, there are apt to be
competing interests.

For instance, in American agriculture, a high price for corn
is good for one type of farmer (the grain farmer), bad for
another (the livestock farmer, who earns more when he can feed
cheap grain), and irrelevant to others (the tobacco farmer, who is
protected by tobacco legislation; or the vegetable farmer, who
needs immigrant labor, and is affected by immigration laws). So
a "sector" of "The Economy," such as agriculture, should also not
be thought of as a single entity, but as a group of sometimes
competing interests, moving at different speeds according to
different motives.

A recent book that illustrates part of this thesis is *Nine
Nations of America,* by Joel Garreau. Garreau's division of the
economy is geographical:[3]

1. New England.
2. The Foundry (New York to Chicago).
3. The Breadbasket (west of Chicago).
4. Dixie.
5. Mex-America (Southern California, Arizona, Texas, and
   Mexico).

6. The Islands (Miami and Eastern Caribbean).
7. Quebec.
8. The Empty Quarter (Utah-Nevada north to Manitoba and Prudhoe Bay, Alaska).
9. Ecotopia (Along the West Coast from San Francisco and Seattle, north to Anchorage).

But each of the geographical divisions is subject to the kind of further disaggregation I mentioned above, with networks of competing sectors and subsectors.

Special interest groups have a bad name today, but there exists nothing except special interests. Each of us has our own interest at heart. Congressional leaders understand this as well as anyone. Constituencies are not homogeneous. They do not speak with one voice, but with contradictory and competing motives. As mentioned before, however, legislators often like to have things both ways.

I once attended a booster session for improved commerce on the Great Lakes, in which it was suggested that better legislation would help. But underneath, it was apparent that each port on the Great Lakes had its own special interest—Cleveland, for instance, wanted to lure coal traffic away from Toledo; Toledo wanted to keep steel traffic away from Chicago; Chicago wanted to keep grain movement away from Duluth, and so on. A Congresswoman from one of the port cities, in whose district lived truck drivers and railroad workers dependent on traffic to the Atlantic and not the Lakes, said she would lead an effort in Congress to get legislation needed to improve things for the Lakes, if the ports could come to her with a *unified* position. Everyone in attendance agreed with her logic, but the unified position proved impossible to achieve. Our special interests won't aggregate into a clean, elegantly structured American Economy.

Introducing complications is tedious, but I hope not thankless. A forest must be cleared before new structures are built. In the next chapter, I will summarize and then address a few possible objections.

Chapter 5

Why Economics Doesn't Work— Summary and Objections

Economics doesn't work because it requires that human affairs yield to science. Economic models are confused with reality, and the result is obfuscation. The language of economics is elaborately euphemistic; it hides plain concepts like greed, hatred, and avarice behind passive concepts like aggregate supply and demand. Every position an economist takes is matchable by an opposite position, and then a hundred in between. Every position is essentially circular, providing connections between data that have no inherent causal relationship.

I further believe that the myth that economics is a science is fostered by a deep-seated psychological need within most of us for certainty in areas where no certainty can be had. Economics doesn't work, but we believe it *should*. If economists provide us with comfort, it is expensive therapy, costing perhaps hundreds of billions of dollars per year (if the oil sector is an example).

Such a sacrifice of wealth to the cause of bringing science where it cannot go will surely mark our century in future histories. But the sacrifice is by no means over yet.

My Theory

1. The demand for answers will always be greater than the supply.
2. Therefore, the price for answers will be high.
3. Therefore, a very large supply of answers will emerge.
4. Therefore, most answers you see will be false, especially when tested against reality.

I can imagine a number of possible reactions and objections to what I have put forth:

OBJECTION 1

First, someone may say, "Look, I know there are difficulties in measuring things, but it all evens out. The sample of things that the government takes isn't accurate in the absolute sense, but the errors are probably spread evenly. There shouldn't be anything wrong with crunching the numbers, as long as you remember that they're averages." To this I would say that the proof should then be in the accuracy of the resulting forecasts, which is nil. The average annual temperature of Lake Erie is 48° Fahrenheit, which should mean it never freezes.

OBJECTION 2

Second, someone a little more exasperated by this dip into the icy waters of indeterminacy might say, "If all you're going to do is tell me that everything is complex, I've got better things to do. I'm not interested. I've got a business to run. I can't stop doing things just because you say we're over-simplifying how complex things are!" To this I say you're the reader I really want, hang on for a minute!

Everything ceases if you don't simplify. The need to reduce reality to simpler models is absolute. Simplification is virtually a property of human life. If you don't agree, ask the nuclear physicist who absent-mindedly bumps into a wall, which according to his latest particle model, is 99 percent vacuum.

OBJECTION 3

Someone might say, "There is nothing *but* models." In fact, this statement was made to me during a meeting in 1986 on the future of world food and population, by Professor Dana Meadows, author of *The Limits to Growth*.

I have already said that human endeavor ceases if you don't simplify. I would agree perhaps that all thought might be considered "modelling" but I doubt that this is a helpful thrust. Modelling with your mind is far different from modelling with an extrasomatic computer.

What I have tried to do in Chapters 2, 3, and 4 is to wake the reader up to the persistence in today's world of confusing *economic* models with reality—especially when these models are elegant, especially when they are larger than their predecessors, and especially when they seem to give psychological comfort against uncertainty.

My message is this: If you keep clearly in mind the concept that *no* model can ever completely *be* reality, then it follows that bigger, more mathematically elaborate models are not necessarily better than smaller ones. Indeed, good models may be qualitative as well as quantitative. If you accept what I argue, then the criterion for judging models is not a scientific nicety, it's the extent to which they make money for you. Nothing more, nothing less.

OBJECTION 4

The most politically cynical of all readers might say, "I agree with you that dedicated econometricians will not read your book, and that even if they do, they will keep on doing what they're doing—but you've neglected the extent to which these dedicated econometricians *already* control the setting of government policy; as they keep at it, it's a self-fulfilling prophecy. Things will become more and more predictable, because policymakers are trying to make it that way. The 'invisible hand' is ever more disappearing every day."

In rebuttal I would cite the Soviets, perhaps the world's premier econometricians and central planners. Why has Soviet crop production been short of target by amounts ranging from 20 percent to 30 percent over the last five or six years? (The same holds for oil production in 1985.) And in the United States, with every economist railing about the danger of federal deficits, why do we continue to set new deficit records? And worldwide, in an era of more and more central planning, how did we produce $1 trillion in essentially unpayable debt by Third World countries? How were the forces of Islam able to quadruple the price of oil, twice? How can truck-bomb drivers be so irrational as to take their own lives in the process? What will happen in the first city held hostage to a stolen or homemade A-bomb?

In other words, it seems to me that the road to world stability is yet rocky, and that reasoning which uses other than a merely scientific approach will lead to better results, especially for those of us interested in struggling to get an extra inch ahead of the competition.

One further amplification: I am not saying that because economics doesn't work, business must fail. Far from it. For the most part, business goes ahead on its own. The resilience of the system of democratic capitalism is largely in the ability of its practitioners (the business leaders) to ignore economics and history anyway. A thousand entrepreneurs try for an opening wide enough for ten; those who succeed are hailed for spotting the opening rather than being the most muscular among the big crowd who saw it. Almost by definition, entrepreneurs don't need economists. My prime target is the executives of mature firms, especially the ones who have economists and who decided to invest $500 billion in oil that cost $40 per barrel in 1981.

Chapter 6

The Nobel Committee versus President Reagan

An attitude of irreverence toward economics is difficult to maintain when all newspapers, sometime in the early autumn, run the front-page story of the year's Nobel Prize winner in economics. Next to the teams of chemists, physicists, and medical doctors—who have further cracked the code of living cells, further demystified the atom, and again saved thousands of lives from disease—there appears an account of what the Nobel selection committee believes to be the most notable achievement in economics. By unspoken convention, the economics prize is accorded the same kind and level of respect as chemistry, physics, and medicine (as opposed to literature and peace). Economics is reported in terms of its "hard" contributions. Literature is much "softer" in terms of its contribution, and ever since the Nobel Peace Prize went to Kissinger for a Vietnam settlement that never took place, peace has been more closely associated with softness, like literature.

In 1981, the Nobel Prize in economics went to Dr. Lawrence Klein of Wharton Econometrics for his contributions in the origin and development of econometrics. In other words, all of the previous chapters of this book would be, in the eyes of the Nobel committee, pure bunk. Having to decide whether the Nobel committee is right and I am wrong is the inescapable burden of life, for which we are all, separately, accountable. Reverence for what most men believe and upon which they bestow honor (and in the case of the Nobel, money) will not always, in fact will rarely, assure any of us a profitable future.

In that fall of 1981, it so happened, I attended a symposium given by the Federal Reserve Bank of Kansas City on "Modelling Agriculture for Policy Analysis in the 1980s," at which Dr. Klein was scheduled to speak. His appearance at this secluded conference in Vail, Colorado, occurred only days after the Nobel Prize was announced, so there was a powerful aura of dignity around him. However, the paper he gave struck me the same way as others I had heard him give, and I was left bewildered about the reality of his award. According to my notes of the meeting, "Larry Klein defines his models, rather grandly I think, as 'approximations of reality'; in my view, his models represent simply a way of quantifying history so that indexes of future economic activity can be mathematically generated. The fact that current models have an abysmal record at predicting these indexes in the future shows that (1) there is more to history than numerical indexes and (2) history is not a deterministic guide to the future."

At least two other speakers held views similar to myself, one a White House aide, the other a former Under Secretary of Agriculture. But they approached Klein rather gingerly, sticking with reasons why the econometric approach is not more widely used than it already is by policymakers, rather than acknowledging that the following are reasons why it should be summarily abandoned:

1. Policymakers must act in a way that leads to staying in office.
2. Time spans for policymakers (for any decisionmakers) are too short and too much influenced by nearby situations to employ long-term models.

3. The path is as important as the destination. Attractive policies must also be achievable via tenable routes.
4. Who wins and who loses is a crucial aspect of American policymaking, and it's not covered by models.
5. Models have misplaced preciseness—it is better to be moderately right in direction than attempt to be correct in magnitude.
6. There is a tidal-wave effect: Policymakers control very few variables and are easily swamped by things not within their control.

The difficulty of keenest interest to me at that time, however, was not mentioned by anyone—namely that business executives cannot relate to solutions and strategies merely on the grounds that "the model says it comes out that way." In other words, the models are so mathematically complex that even their authors, with or without a Nobel Prize, cannot explain them, but can only keep repeating what the assumptions were and what the final printout says.

About two years after the Nobel Prize was awarded to Klein, another prominent public figure joined the debate on the value of economics, and although not every reader here will put him in the same league as the Nobel committee, he is clearly a man to be reckoned with.

"I hope you'll keep in mind that economic forecasting is far from a perfect science. If recent history is any guide, the experts have some explaining to do about what they told us had to happen but never did," said President Ronald Reagan in January of 1984.

And a few months later, the President's Chief of Staff, Donald Regan, blurted out a blunt, "Who needs 'em?" in reference to the President's Council of Economic Advisers, whose 330-page annual report warned about the danger of the Administration's budget deficits. Members of the President's Council of Economic Advisers are considered the highest ranking of all gurus, but the Reagan White House steadfastly ignored them, and as the big-name economists resigned one by one, new appointments were not forthcoming. Hints were dropped that the Council would be discarded. Professional economists everywhere in the country were incensed. They did not say so, but it was clear that the biggest customer of all for economic advice was calling their bluff. What they said instead was that the Administration was getting rid of anyone who does not agree with it.

In April of 1985, the White House finally gave in and appointed a new Chief Economist to the Council, Beryl W. Sprinkel. Sprinkel had already been a part of the Administration, in Treasury, and was apparently prepared not to bother the President unduly with the results of his analyses. According to an interview given the *Chicago Tribune* in October 1985, Sprinkel said that he had Reagan's ear to provide economic advice, although he added that "the President is his own chief economic adviser." And further, "He has a degree in economics, you know, and his grasp of situations is amazing."[1]

I will not here take sides for or against Ronald Reagan's political agenda. I will observe, however, that those of us who accept the direct responsibility for being our own chief economic adviser are not only being courageous but also realistic and mature. Executives accountable for practical results cannot really duck behind the advice of others; they may try, but it won't wash forever, and their progress will be limited.

Why, then, aren't more government administrators and business executives taking Reagan's lead? Why don't businessmen, in particular, scrap a practice that costs so much and produces so little? Businessmen are closer to a "laboratory" than government officials; businessmen have the test of the marketplace. In fact, whether they want it or not, the market gives immediate feedback to inaccurate forecasts, in the form of red ink. What would be wrong with a chief executive saying, "I'm only going to pay for advice that helps me to be right in the marketplace. That will be all the comfort I need. I'm going to stop pretending that someone can model the future with computers, and I'm going to accept responsibility for being right—at least for being more right than my competition."

Chapter 7

Changing Our Outlook

The changes in outlook I am recommending were conceived in the context of business, in fact of a rather large business, with a chief executive and a corporate economist. The changes are still most easily explained in this big-company context, but their applicability is broad. If you are both your own chief executive and your own chief economist, then the following changes will be just as beneficial for you as for the functionaries I am rhetorically addressing.

The changes I recommend are in one sense massive but in another sense small. For instance, I do not recommend that we entirely do away with experts, or with computers. Instead, I argue that if both we and our experts will change our philosophical outlook, we will together stand a much greater chance of beating the competition in this present age of uncertainty.

The idea that people should change their entire philosophy is, of course, overwhelming. But it may not be as hard as it sounds. The new philosophy that I propose is not totally unfamiliar. I have seen cases in which the switch has been made as soon as it was recognized that the option was available.

In other words, my new position is by no means unnatural; in fact, I would argue that the thing that is most unnatural is the belief that a business executive, in order to make the most profitable decisions, must be presented with the Truth about economic conditions in his future markets—and that this Truth can actually be obtained by scientific data processing of numerical indexes in computer models.

What the executive must do is to accept full and total responsibility for decisions and for the knowledge required to make them sound. What the chief researcher must do is abandon the forecasting of Truth (guruism) and adopt the role of adjutant to the executive whom he serves, closely supporting that person's pursuit of fuller knowledge.

The cornerstone of the failure of economists has been the mistaken view that knowledge does not exist in persons, but only in books, data tables, and computers. Real knowledge exists only in real people. Businesspeople succeed according to whether they have full and accurate knowledge of situations. The knowledge they possess is contained in their own minds, nowhere else. They may have been helped in the formation of that knowledge by written reports, charts, memos, and so on, but it is only what they fully incorporate in their minds that makes up their living knowledge.

The principle that the human mind is primary has long been a part of formal philosophy. Let me quote from the nineteenth-century philosopher John Henry Newman:

> Great as are the services of language in enabling us to extend the compass of our inferences, to test their validity, and to communicate with others, still the mind itself is more versatile and vigorous than any of its works. . . . It determines what science cannot determine, the limit of converging probabilities and the reasons sufficient for a proof. . . . Nor is it by any diagram that we are able to scrutinize, sort, and combine the many premises which must be first run together before we can answer duly a given question. It is to the living mind that we must look for the means of using correctly principles of whatever kind, facts or doctrines, experiences or testimonies, true or probable, and of discerning what conclusion from these is necessary, suitable or expedient.[1]

Today's businessman knows very well that his decisions are as much affected by rumor, hearsay, and gossip as by detailed study of facts and logic. Newman understood this. In 1878, Newman listed "tradition, analogy, isolated monuments and records, ruins, vague reports, legends, the facts or sayings of later times, language, and proverbs"[2] as part of the array of methods that the mind must sort through in building genuine knowledge. But today's business executives feel compelled to hide from this. They seek to appear "rational" at all costs, to such an extreme that they deny their own humanity, along with their potential to enhance profits. They are often at conflict within themselves, trying to reconcile what they believe in their heart and soul and what someone is telling them they *should* believe, on the basis of some or another economic model.

The economist, especially the econometrician, has in essence been telling the executive, "You're a dummy. You can't possibly know all there is to know. You certainly can't begin to know, in your head, all the economic factors I've got modelled in this 1,000-equation package." Strictly speaking, the economist is right, but that is irrelevant. What the economist has in the package is not knowledge but chess. The game of chess is ruthlessly logical; it will thus be no surprise one day when computers beat the best living players. Logic, not knowledge, is the province of computers. Chess does not require knowledge, in the truest sense; it requires elaborate logic. Personnel departments are not instructed to recruit business candidates from chess clubs; if a top business executive happens to be a chess master, that is a coincidence.

Let me continue further with the eminence of the single human mind, and by way of an example introduce a term for the intellectual function of crucial importance to success in business. The example comes from comparing business with warfare (which is much more fruitful than comparing it with chess). Suppose Napoleon is on a hill, surveying the coming battle. He has toured his own troops and has them stationed where he wants them. He is now studying the terrain and the position of the enemy. After a few minutes, during which he has remained silent, he points to a wooded area down the hill on his right and says, "We'll attack through the woods at dawn." His lieutenants prepare to carry the order to the troops. They have just watched the great general apply a lifetime's worth of knowledge to a particular situation, and they are willing to bet their lives that his knowledge is the best available.

The faculty that Napoleon exercised in this example is called the illative sense, which uses the entirety of our reasoning faculty. This is not the same as intuition, nor is it what is usually meant by "gut feeling." The illative sense involves genuine reasoning, taking into account not only logic and a lifetime of previous experiences, but new information, scouting reports, topography, and so on. Intuition and gut feelings are usually applied when one is operating without sufficient facts. The illative sense makes use not only of facts but also of the full array of evidence and of previous experience.

A crucial fact about the illative sense, from the standpoint of my own arguments, is that its operation will not usually be illuminable by its owner. In other words, a good general may not be able to explain the details of *why* the march should proceed in a certain manner, he simply *knows* that it should. The belief, "If you can't explain it well, you must not know it well," is wrong. It is a damaging misunderstanding of the illative sense. In fact, forcing a competent executive to explain himself to the nth degree will usually interrupt the illative sense and destroy its soundness—especially if the executive subscribes to the fallacy that living knowledge can be fully explained to others.

Suppose one of Napoleon's lieutenants has scouted the woods. He says to the general, "Sir, I have been partway into the woods. There is a stream with no fords, so perhaps we should carry timbers with us." Or, "I have prepared a map of the woods, showing the pathways and streams." If the general and his lieutenant then join together in careful scrutiny of the map, it can happen that the general's illative sense will be enabled to make a more fully informed decision about the battle than before. This is the type of partnership that the executive and his chief researcher should seek.

But before elaborating on how to carry out this kind of partnership, let me summarize the reasons once again for seeking to undertake it. Changes in outlook are required both by the executive and by the chief researcher, which is the generic label I've chosen for the former position of corporate economist. Figure 7-1 is addressed to the executive and Figure 7-2 to the researcher; they summarize the philosophical changes necessary to a new partnership. The reader should study each of the figures (on pp. 55–56) before continuing.

The key to each figure is recognition of where, for business, the "standard of Truth" lies. It lies in the market. Whatever the executive does should help earn more profits from the market and provide greater longevity for the firm. Whatever the chief researcher does should further the executive's ability to earn money from the market. This may sound incredibly elementary, but it nonetheless requires all the emphasis possible.

Truth with a capital "T" cannot be achieved in forecasting markets. What can be achieved is the ability to come a fraction closer to the truth than your competitors and to arrive there sooner. The function of forecasting is the executive's, not the researcher's. The researcher can provide maps that may help the executive see how things work and thus improve the potential of the illative sense to do a better job than the competitor's. But neither the executive nor the researcher should confuse the maps with reality; the reality that matters to profits is what the executive *knows,* not what is in the computer.

The test of the new relationship between executive and researcher is the market. The chief executive asks about the research, "Does it give me more confidence in configuring my assets?" and with time, "Are my assets more profitable than they were, considering my competition and considering prevailing conditions?" The marketing manager (or the trader or the sales manager or the finance manager) asks, "Does the research give me new concepts that allow me to adapt to daily realities in the marketplace faster and more accurately than my competition can adapt?"

The following chapters will amplify the new partnership

(text continues on p. 56)

Figure 7–1. Changes in outlook required by top managements for successful strategy without economists.

Abandon the View that:	Adopt the View that:
Truth is possible.	Getting minutely closer to Truth than the competition is possible.
I am the guru. They should follow my forecasts.	My forecasts are usually wrong. Managers can and do make their own forecasts, and then must live with them. How can I help them be rational while still supporting their inner, experiencial grasp of their markets?
Forecasts should be made with many scenarios, so that all the eventualities are covered.	Managers already know the possibilities. They need concepts that will help them see the most likely scenario before their competition sees it.
What matters is the position I take, and whether I am right.	I should take positions more to illustrate how my arguments work than to convince others to follow me.
Quantitative analysis underpins everything.	In our present Age of Uncertainty, qualitative analysis is usually more important than quantitative—often because competitors aren't doing it well. The techniques of critical history and literary criticism offer big potentials for objectivity.
The substance of a forecast is more important than its form.	Form and substance are equal. Presentation is 50 percent of the job. High-quality graphics and clear writing are key.
Strategies must be founded on forecasts of the Truth.	To support step-like, modular strategies, managers need a systematic way of continually monitoring external intelligence, along with creative yet realistic concepts of integration.

Figure 7–2. Changes in outlook required by the chief researcher for successful strategy without economists.

Abandon the View that:	*Adopt the View that:*
Truth is possible.	Getting minutely closer to Truth than the competition is possible.
Economics is a science.	Economics is a child of politics and culture. Human nature cannot be plumbed by science alone.
Economic gurus are responsible for forecasting Truth.	Managers are responsible for forecasting. To win, they need teachers and systematic methods rather than faith.
Econometric models will one day succeed, given smart enough computers and large enough data bases.	Simple models, limited to two or three variables at a time, may help managers understand markets and do their job of forecasting better.
The economy can be known by mathematically integrating all its indicators.	"The Economy" is a fiction. The economy is really millions of separate people and companies, with conflicting goals, not capable of being measured.
Economics is the lead discipline in forecasting.	Quantitative history sets the context for forecasting, followed by the other humanities, especially clear writing and criticism. Simplified economics has a role.
Strategies must be founded on forecasts of the Truth.	Strategies should be designed in step-like and modular fashion so that, as systematic monitoring reveals Change, strategies can be adapted *faster by one's own company than by the competition.*

available to executive and researcher if they change their outlooks. There are serious pitfalls—"Napoleon" may be too arrogant to listen to an adjutant—but there are offsetting tools, methods, and principles that will help make the partnership prosper.

And in the end there is an implication for business strategy itself, which I call modular. Inasmuch as the future cannot be predicted, strategy should be designed in step-like and modular fashion so that, as systematic monitoring reveals change, strategies can be adapted by one's own firm more quickly than by the competition.

Chapter 8

Irreverence, Nonsense, and Myth

The required changes in outlook will come easily to some, not so easily to others. To discover where you may fall in this range, answer the following questions.

MAKING THE CHANGE—WHERE ARE YOU NOW?

Question: You pick up the Sunday paper and glance at the business section. What would your reaction be to the following comment by a New York economist in an article about the economic outlook in 1986? "The American consumer is overextended. A broadly based buying binge—exacerbated by this summer's tantalizingly cheap car loans—in the face of inadequate income growth has put tremendous pressure on the household sector."

Answer: "Caution. This statement is not in plain language. It sounds complex and cumbersome." Or even more severely, "Could this statement be nonsense?"

I am not advocating public irreverence, but private. I am not urging that you telephone the author and shout, "Baloney!" I am saying that for the sake of better profits you should be willing quietly to take on any statement by any economist anywhere, and unmask it privately, for your own benefit.

The clue to the above quotation is in the language. Just as "The Economy" doesn't exist, neither does "The American Consumer." Precisely what is "overextended?" What is a "broadly based buying binge?" What is "tremendous pressure?" Who is *not* in the "household sector?" The language tells you that this economist is talking within the framework of a model. He is not telling you something of which he has genuine knowledge, he's telling you how he has it econometrically modelled.

One of the best ways for both executive and researcher to exercise their objectivity is with irreverence. When something sounds like it may be nonsense, say so—at least privately. When language is artificial, say so—write it down in red on the clipping as you read. This is not something that another person can do for you. Your skepticism must be your own.

Continuing with the test of your change in outlook, here's a second question: The time is June 1985. You come across a double-full-page ad in *The New York Times* that reads, "To the Senate and House Conference Committees: BUDGET CUTS NOW. THEN TAX REFORM." It is signed by the founding members of the Bipartisan Budget Appeal, who are five former Secretaries of the Treasury, and one former Secretary of Commerce. Hundreds of other notable persons have also signed. What should be your reaction to the message of the ad, given below?

> The President and Congress have at last acknowledged the scale of our budgetary imbalance, have discarded the notion that we could "grow our way out," and have acted to reduce the severe economic risks of $200 billion plus deficits "as far as the eye can see." But action is incomplete, the hour late, and the damage mounting fast: Economic warning signals are already flashing (the anemic .7 percent economic growth of the first quarter); real interest rates remain at unprecedented levels that strain and destabilize our financial system; the dollar remains massively overvalued as a result of the unprecedented capital flows needed to balance our national accounts; the spiraling growth of federal debt continues to undermine long-run economic confidence by

placing monetary authorities in an excruciating bind. The House and Senate Budget Resolutions are an impressive start, but action is now imperative. We urge all concerned Americans to let the conferees, the leadership of both chambers, and the President know that courage, compromise, and a comprehensive deficit-reduction plan are urgent and imperative.[1]

What is your reaction?
Answer: "Sounds like they're *selling* rather than explaining."
Keep in mind two things: (1) Patriotic rhetoric and emotional cliche will often overshadow fact, and (2) it is not unpatriotic to be irreverent, in private, if it feeds your objectivity and improves your profits.

The above advertisement in the *Times* tips its hand, once again, by its language; though it is not econometric-ese, it is almost entirely couched in emotional cliche. It is meant to rally support, not provide objective explanation. I'm sure that as you read it, even if you basically agreed with the premise that the deficit is at the root of all our problems, you also felt a little skepticism arise as the authors heat the issue up.

Suppose we remove the emotion. Let me try to restate in clear, objective prose the argument for the budget deficit as the central cause of all economic problems:

> The government deficit must be financed in competition with all other borrowers, from a fixed pool of savings. This crowds out other borrowers and drives up interest rates. Higher interest rates make the dollar strong, which hurts exports. The overvalued dollar also increases imports, thus hurting domestic employment and pulling down overall GNP.

Now what's your reaction?
Answer: "Doesn't square with the facts."
I don't expect this exercise to be easy. Skepticism is something of a forgotten virtue in America today. The lack of it, in fact, is the reason for this book. My position on the budget-deficit argument is that, as logical as the argument sounds, it doesn't turn out to be true. *It doesn't agree with the facts.*

Study the following data carefully:

Year	Federal Deficit (in Billions)	90-Day T-Bill Interest Rate
1980	$ 60	11.0%
1981	60	14.0
1982	111	10.5
1983	195	9.0
1984	175	11.0
1985	212	8.0

According to the above figures, what has happened? The federal deficit has climbed from $60 billion in 1980 to $212 billion in 1985, during which time interest rates (as typified by Treasury bills) began at 11 percent, peaked at 14 percent, and then *declined to 8 percent.* How then can it be asserted that the deficits are causing high interest rates? Interest rates have gone *down,* not up.

I would be pleased if at this point the majority of readers said, "But you almost had me convinced not to believe *any* data, and now you want to build a case yourself with somebody else's data!" If this was your reaction, I want to apologize for over-emphasis; I am not advocating the abandonment of data, not at all; I am urging the use of data within the limits of its own accuracy, and for purposes that illuminate rather than conceal things from the illative sense. In the immediate case, the data are actually quite reliable. The federal deficit is just the balance of the government checking account(s), after all disbursements have been made; it is subject to error, of course, and to the judgment involved in all accounting matters, but as indicators go, it is relatively reliable. A "final" deficit figure of $200 billion might be correct to within plus or minus 10 billion—a satisfactory range for the argument under study. Likewise, the interest rate on Treasury bills is determined by public auction and is recorded by the New York Fed and published daily. There is, once again, some error—not just from human blunders in writing things down but in the differences between the "bid" and "asked prices" at various times during an accounting period. I would estimate, however, than an interest rate of 10 percent might be good to plus or minus .125 percent—once again a small enough range not to confuse the present argument. My previous examples of large, inherent data problems focussed on aggregate indicators, such as GNP and trade balance; these are usually accompanied by explicit "errors and omissions" ranges provided by the data's authors. What we are discussing here is an important part of knowledge, called *critical history*, which is explored more fully in Chapter 11. For the moment, let's agree that the final published figures on the budget deficit and interest rates are reasonably good.

LET'S FACE FACTS

According to reliable data, in the past several years as the deficit has risen interest rates have fallen. This is the truth, or as close as we can come. Yet most executives I know have disallowed these facts. If you're having trouble accepting them, please turn to Figure 8–1, and study it. The figure charts the deficit and actual interest rates from 1970 to 1985. Study the two lines, looking for correlations, expecially from 1980 to 1985. As the deficit line rises, what happens to the interest rate line? Does it rise as well? I think that if you look at the graph long enough, you will see that *higher deficits have meant lower interest rates*.

The urge to believe that the facts are wrong and that the "other way" must be right is so strong that the reader looking at Figure 8–1 will immediately start creating excuses. The most popular one is, "It's a temporary aberration." The second most

Figure 8–1. As the federal deficit increased sharply in 1982 and 1983, T-bill interest rates declined.

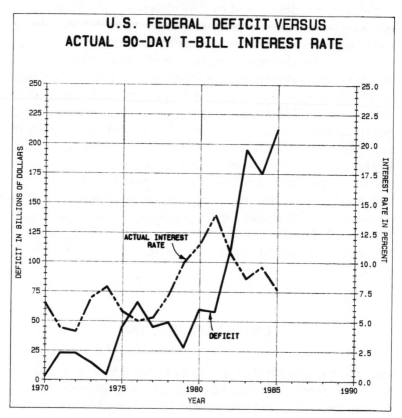

Source: **U.S. Department of Commerce.**

popular is, "There were lots of other things happening at the same time."

To the first excuse I reply: How can reality be an aberration without being reality, especially when it has gone on for four years or more?

The second excuse, concerning a combination of factors instead of a straight link, is more difficult to dismiss. To solve the difficulty, economists have created a concept called *real interest rate,* illustrated in Figures 8–2 and 8–3. The first of these two figures plots both interest rate data and inflation rate data. (The data on inflation are much more subject to error than interest rates, but let's ignore that for the moment, to see where the argument leads.)

The *difference* between the two lines in Figure 8–2 is called the real interest rate, and it is plotted as a separate quantity in Figure 8–3. The argument is that an investor who is evaluating a given interest rate will take into consideration what the inflation rate is in making an investment decision. In other words, if an Argentine bond pays 15 percent interest, that seems pretty attractive; but if inflation in Argentina is running at 30 percent, the bond looks worthless. After one year an investor would have gained 15 percent payments but lost 30 percent of the face value, because the purchasing power of the peso keeps going down.

Those in favor of using "real" interest rates like to refer to actual rates as "nominal." Presumably this is to stop you from wondering how "real" rates can be more real than "actual." It is easy, they must think, to see that "real" is more real than "nominal," so they re-label things. This linguistic trickery is the heart and substance not only of modern economics but of human endeavor itself; it is a clue to how man has masked reality from himself so many times over the centuries. In other words, in my view, we must treat the notion of real interest rates with real skepticism.

First of all, as shown in Figure 8–3, how could it have happened that real interest rates were *negative* for several years in the early 1970s? Actual (nominal) rates were not negative, of course; only "real" ones were. You could not have negative

Figure 8–2. The difference between actual interest rate (on 90-day T-bills) and inflation is called "real" interest rate by economists.

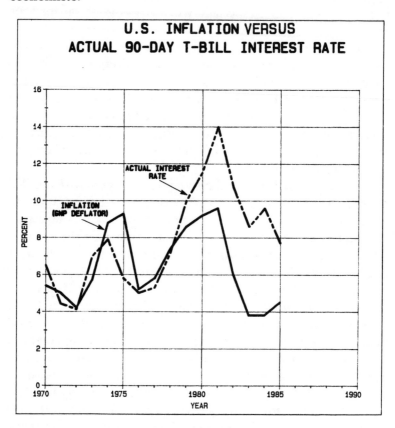

Source: U.S. Department of Commerce.

Figure 8–3. "Real" interest rate is calculated by subtracting inflation rate from actual interest rate on 90-day T-bills.

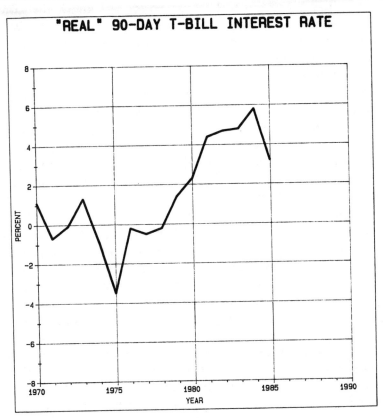

Source: U.S. Department of Commerce.

interest rates, in the strict sense, and still have continuity of ownership in banking and commerce. The bank owners did not literally pay borrowers to borrow. So far as I know, the early 1970s did not fall into some kind of Black Hole; that is, bankers and other capitalists all made profits as before, all made investments, all ate well, and so on.

At this point, the proponents of real rates will say that what they really mean is to construct a rate than subtracts the *expectation* of inflation (in the future) from the nominal rates that are occurring at the same time as the expectations. The proponents say that using inflation as it was recorded after it happened is not the same as considering expectations. I heartily agree. But how do you measure expectations? How do you measure someone's beliefs about the future?

The measurement problem in this last case is different from the ones we've discussed, and far from being a tedious detail, it is at the core of the double-think being committed. The proponents of real interest rates will go so far as to say, "Yes, you're right, you can't measure expectations. You have to use the actual recorded values of inflation as *proxies* for the expectations." In other words, real is a proxy for unreal? If you cannot measure something, do you use what is already measured and pretend that it gives you what you wanted of the unknown? So desperate is the modeller to get on with the model that he will replace "actual" with a concept called *expected,* and, when that proves impossible to measure, he will then use "actual" as a proxy for expected.

WHAT ABOUT IMMEASURABILITY?

Immeasurability is an unpopular subject in today's world. If you claim that something cannot be measured, you are seen as being irksome; if you persist, you will simply be circumvented. "Pay someone else to go measure it," a manager might say; "I don't care how you do it, just get it done, and bring me the data." The imperative is to get on with the business at hand in a scientific way. If measurements are required, get them. If measurements are difficult, get clever—find indirect proxies that *can* be measured. The business decisionmaking process, it would seem, can only work if you feed it numbers.

So the idea flourishes that anything can be proxied. People's expectations of future inflation can be proxied by actual inflation at the present time. If you take actual interest rates and subtract the rate of inflation (the proxy), you get real interest rates. To be convinced that the deficit causes real interest rates to rise, see Figure 8–4. There seems to me little doubt that the two lines in Figure 8–4 are moving together most of the time, with notable exceptions. A statistical regression test indicates that the deficit explains high real interest rates in about two-thirds of the cases ($R^2 = .68$). Is this conclusive evidence that the conjunction of various forces provides a suitable way out of the straightforward problem with which we began—namely, that on the surface actual interest rates have gone *down* the more the deficit has risen?

Economic forces can and do act in conjunction with each other. You cannot single out a factor and see its results in isolation. In the complicated world of reality, forces are often cumulative. In other words, if both inflation and interest rates are rising at previously unheard of rates, that's bad, and you would expect the economic impact to hit at least twice as hard. I am not rejecting the notion that many forces are acting at once; but in 1985, (1) interest rates were falling, and this was seen as good, and (2) inflation rates were falling, and this too was seen as good. How can two good things come out bad? In other words, it will be easy to believe in the additive nature of two troublesome factors, like rising interest and rising inflation. It will be difficult to believe that when the same two factors are heading toward improvement the differential rate of improvement will itself cause a major headache, in this case a rise in the dollar. It is as if two very naughty children were teaming up to cause trouble; the parents of each take them to their respective homes; both

Figure 8–4. Whether or not "real" interest rate and federal deficit are correlated is a matter of opinion. Someone analyzing the statistics might say, "Yes, they are somewhat correlated." A person simply looking at the graph might say, "They're correlated, but not 100 percent. Sometimes interest rates go down when they 'should' go up."

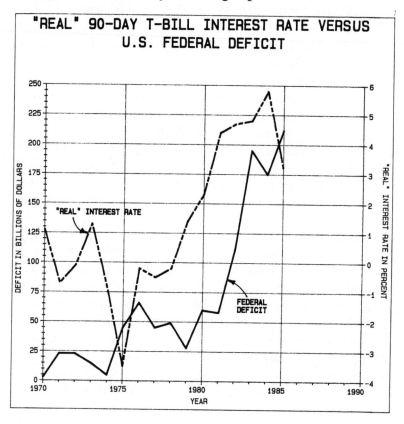

Source: U.S. Department of Commerce.

children begin to behave much better, but one a little more slowly than the other; how can this differential have anywhere near the force of their joint perversity?

APPLYING IRREVERENCE

The three or four factors considered in this chapter, when correlated statistically, give regression results at which a physical scientist would scoff. "Two-thirds of the cases? You can't build technology that works only two-thirds of the time." But if the econometric modeller throws in enough other indicators and tries multiple correlations, better R^2s will eventually appear, because all indicators belong to one big economic family. Indicators have things in common. It is like going to a big family picnic. At some point, everyone arrives, everyone eats and drinks, everyone joins in the ballgame, everyone eats the watermelon, and everyone leaves—all within some measurable tolerance. But to take a particular person at the picnic (say the deficit) and to claim that her recent growth spurt will cause a cousin (say interest rates) to gain weight is at best tenuous. When the cousin is *not* gaining weight, but in fact losing, then the argument should be abandoned altogether.

Take another look at Figure 8–4. Either you believe what you see there, or you don't. The only other recourse is a printout of the statistical indicators themselves. It is the reader's decision to make. Is there enough evidence in front of your eyes to convince you that real interest is more real than actual?

That's not an easy question. Your answer depends a great deal on your philosophy. If you believe that human affairs are mechanistic, that each of us is an economic unit with a supply-and-demand chip for a brain and that emotions don't count, then it should indeed be possible to aggregate billions of such units in a large enough computer. If, on the other hand, you believe that human affairs are not fully rational, that each of us has free choice, then it won't be possible to sum us all up, because too frequently the "normal" way we behave will be interrupted by freedom, by accident, by foolishness, or by genius. Taking this latter route enables me to look at Figure 8–4 and say, "That's part of it. There's a shadow there of the way things really are. But it's not a display of causes, it's a display of results. I cannot make my best forecast by expecting the indicators themselves to predict future indicators; I must use all the broad philosophical understanding at my command to predict future indicators."

When I have displayed the facts on deficit and interest rates to live audiences, the reaction is often, "Here is some lunatic trying to prove that the deficit doesn't matter!" My answer is that the deficit very definitely matters, but not in the way most people think. I believe that the causal connections that most economists *claim* exist between the deficit and interest rates and other indicators simply cannot be shown in a way that would help me help managers make more money. The behavior of interest rates in the markets has been contrary to what economists have predicted. I say, therefore, on this very simple evidence, "Toss out those models and find something that works better in the market."

Nevertheless, the deficit continues to matter because people *believe* it matters. It can be seen with a simple graph that it is a myth that high deficits are always accompanied by high interest rates. But in terms of the national political agenda, that is entirely irrelevant. Most people continue to believe that the deficit does cause high interest rates, and that's what matters.

People believe myths. They always have. This is not irreverence, but history. The approach I'm recommending in this book is to drop one myth, but not to underestimate what myths can do. I am recommending that we drop the myth that economic models can forecast the future and make us money; I am arguing that our own mind can be developed into a much more sure source of profitable judgments; I am saying that this can happen if we are willing to (privately) apply irreverence, test myths with facts, and proceed according to our illative sense, with great respect for (among other things) the role of myths in human affairs.

Chapter 9

Quantitative History

Whatever happens tomorrow will be new. It will never have happened before. But it will be *like* what has happened before. And for this reason, history cannot be ignored. Nothing much seems to change from one day to the next. But after about two months, many things have changed. And after a couple of years, everything has changed.

IDENTIFYING HISTORICAL TRENDS

Daily analysis, as in stock market reports, commodities bulletins, and newspaper articles, tends to obscure the underlying trends of history. A *trend* is some large movement that, when it becomes history, will have affected the capital assets of business. If a trend goes unnoticed, chief executives, after a couple of years have passed, will wish that they had reconfigured their assets to maximize the trend's positive effects or to avoid its adversity.

The early detection of new trends and of changes in the speed of old ones is an important job for our illative sense. Whatever can be done to improve our ability to see the trends of the market better and faster than our competition should be pursued to the utmost.

What I recommend is that we become willing to devote a larger share of our study time explicitly to reading history, rather than to reading contemporary books that advance theories, use economic models, and demonstrate only a casual understanding of history itself. The approach to history that I suggest could be called scholarly, as opposed to popular or anecdotal. It is not necessarily dry and tedious, but it is characterized by extreme attention to the correctness of sources, to details of events, and to objective interpretation.

The kind of study I'm recommending can be divided along three avenues:

1. Quantitative history (discussed in this chapter).
2. Narrative history (see Chapter 10).
3. Critical history (see Chapter 11).

Quantitative history asks "How can trends be delineated?" The key word is *delineated*—how can trends be shown as lines?

USING CRITICAL ANALYSIS TO DELINEATE TRENDS

As an example of a trend we would like to better delineate, let us take the claim that, "The present is more uncertain than the past, and is becoming ever more so." Can this claim be delineated, and in the process tested and verified?

Uncertainty is usually associated with unpredictable change, with volatility that cannot be insured against by some business action. For instance, you cannot buy insurance, as such, to guard against the swings up and down of U.S. gross national product. Nor can you purchase insurance to protect against inflation or interest rate changes. You can minimize your risk by using the interest rate options now available on various mercantile exchanges, and the relatively recent creation of such options is in a way testament to the uncertainty surrounding these factors. It must be realized, however, that the options markets do not reduce uncertainty; in fact, the options would not work unless sufficiently large numbers of investors and speculators had opposing opinions on how the trends were headed.

Figure 9-1 shows the change in the annual percent of U.S. gross national product. The annual percent change is one measure of the "volatility" of our national economy, taken in aggregate. Various sectors of the economy could also be shown in the same way, but let us stay with the aggregate to illustrate what is meant by quantitative history and what the importance of "historical context" is in delineating trends.

Figure 9-1, in displaying the volatility of GNP from 1960 to 1984, presents inconclusive data. It might be argued that the decade of the 1960s appears slightly more stable than the 1970s and 1980s, but such a conclusion is not readily supported by the graph. My rule is that if a graph's message is not obvious, ignore it. It might be necessary for the graph's author to tour the observer around, pointing things out with labels—but the reader should be skeptical and should not have to imagine the presence of unseen factors. We should strive to find only that which is evident, not that which the expert believes is there but is not readily visible.

Figure 9-2 puts the data in more of a historical context than Figure 9-1 does. We can now see the volatility of GNP for seven and a half decades. What is obvious from this graph? Most observers would say that GNP was much more volatile in the 1920s, 1930s, and 1940s than it has been since then. So if there is a trend toward uncertainty, we cannot use the volatility of aggregate GNP to delineate it. Evidently, the country has been able to avoid major wars (like World War I and World War II), and the country in total has enjoyed smoother growth since the 1950s—perhaps due to political policies of the federal government, perhaps not. The graph quantifies the volatility but does not necessarily explain the causes. Associating causes with points and lines is another avenue of history, to be taken up in the next chapter.

Figure 9-3 shows the volatility of inflation in the period 1960 to 1984. Unlike our previous illustrations on GNP, it would seem obvious from the graph of Figure 9-3 that the volatility of inflation is increasing. But let us add more historical context. Turn to Figure 9-4. Viewed over seven and a half

Figure 9–1. This graph is inconclusive. It is difficult to tell
whether U.S. GNP has been more volatile in recent years
than it was in the 1960s.

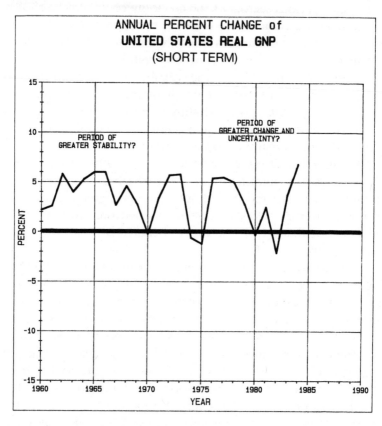

Source: Council of Economic Advisers.

Figure 9–2. This graph is more illuminating than Figure 9–1; a larger historical context changes one's perception of relative uncertainty. U.S. GNP was much more volatile before the 1950s than after.

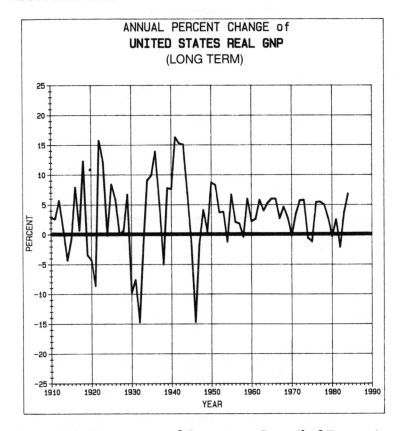

Source: U.S. Department of Commerce; Council of Economic Advisers.

Figure 9–3. The consumer price index is certainly higher in the 1970s than the 1960s, but do we have a good enough historical context in this graph to reach a valid conclusion?

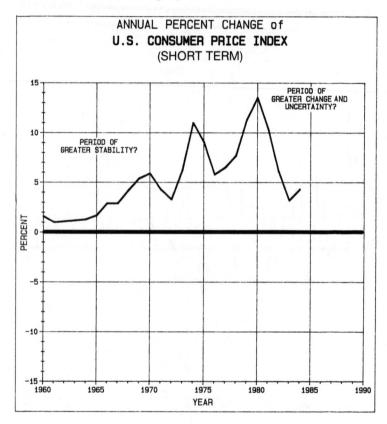

Source: **Council of Economic Advisers.**

Figure 9–4. Once again, looking at a larger time span changes our view. Consumer prices were very high in both periods of wartime prior to the 1950s.

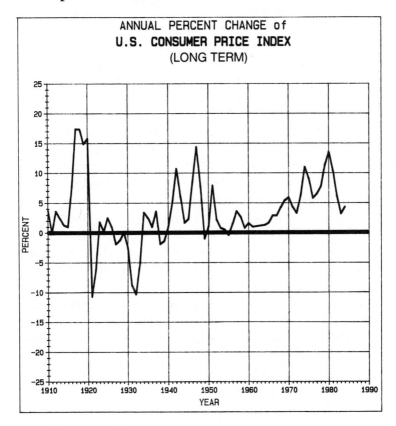

Source: U.S. Department of Commerce; Council of Economic Advisers.

decades, inflation in the 1970s looks less unusual. Both wartime periods were extremely volatile, as were the early 1930s.

What about interest rates? Study Figure 9-5, which shows the average annual Federal Reserve Bank discount rate. This figure peaked in 1981. Have interest rates become more uncertain and volatile? Examine Figure 9-6, which puts the data in a historical context. Conclusion? The long-term graph shows, I think, that interest rates in the 1970s were *higher* than at any time in the previous six decades, and this is surely testament to uncertainty in the climate for business. Bankers were not willing to loan money except for a higher premium; things must have looked less certain to them.

But higher rates are not necessarily the same as more volatile rates. The graph of Figure 9-6 is not a graph of volatility but of magnitude. It plots the actual size of rates, which happens to be expressed as percent, and not the annual percent change in the rate. If we are attempting to arrive at some conclusion about where the uncertainty in the present age lies, then we must be sure to compare our factors on the basis of "apples to apples and oranges to oranges."

Figure 9-7 gives the annual percent change of interest rates, and it is consistent with the method used in Figures 9-2 and 9-4, which charted GNP and inflation. Once again our perception changes. The *volatility* of interest rates in the last few years is not that much different from what has occurred over previous decades. If this is true, then we have narrowed our definition of the Age of Uncertainty to mean "a time of higher average annual interest rates."

Let's drop down from the national aggregate to an example of one sector of the economy, agricultural exports. The front pages of newspapers have been full of articles about problems with U.S. farming and exports. Have agricultural exports become more uncertain and volatile lately? Examine Figure 9-8, which shows the annual percent change in U.S. agricultural exports since 1910. According to the graph, volatility in this sector was greater during both world wars, and even in the 1950s, than it is today. What then is the problem?

Go to Figure 9-9. The problem is magnitude, not volatility.

Figure 9–5. Interest rates are clearly higher in the present decade than in the 1960s. What's in store for the remainder of the century?

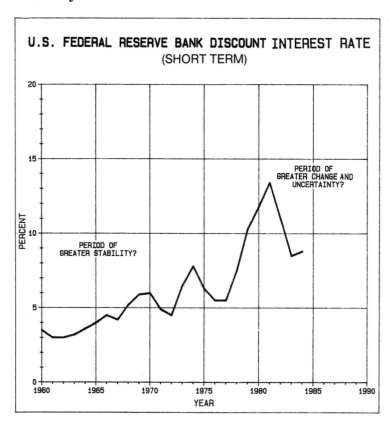

Source: Council of Economic Advisers.

Figure 9–6. Interest rates are indeed higher today than at any time in the past century. Money lenders and borrowers alike must believe that we live in a more risky climate now than in the past.

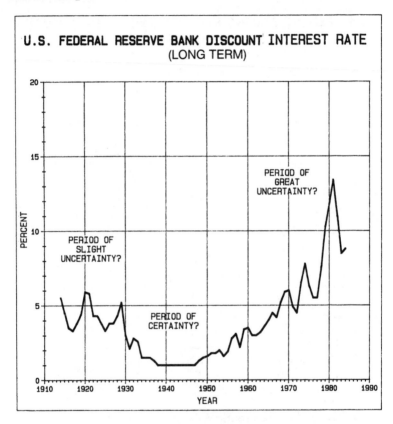

Source: **U.S. Department of Commerce; Council of Economic Advisers.**

Figure 9–7. The previous chart (Figure 9–6) showed the *magnitude* of interest rates; this chart shows their *volatility*. The volatility of interest rates in recent years is not unusual when compared with volatility over the past century, but the magnitude is. Using consistent methods of comparison changes our perception of uncertainty.

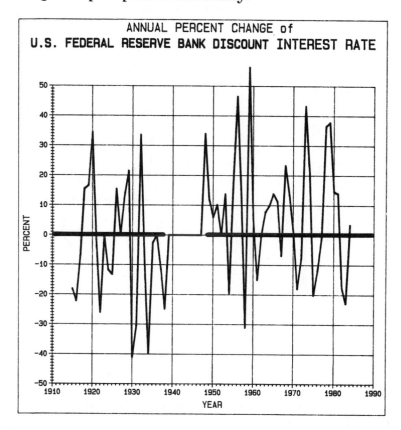

Source: U.S. Department of Commerce; Council of Economic Advisers.

Figure 9–8. The volatility of U.S. agricultural exports
appears to have decreased in recent years. Why then is our
farm sector hurting so badly? Annual percent change may not
capture the cumulative effect of change.

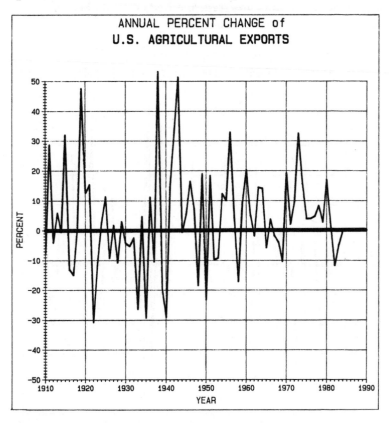

Source: U.S. Department of Commerce; Council of Economic
Advisers.

Figure 9-9. The farm sector is hurting because of the decline of exports from their *cumulative peak.* Thus we see that the quantitive history of uncertainty must include both magnitude and volatility. Showing cumulative growth in the 1970s alters the perception provided by the chart of annual percent change.

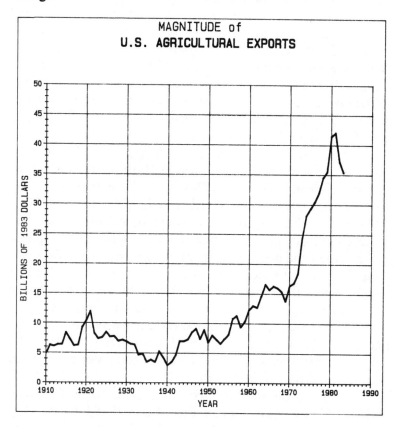

Source: U.S. Department of Commerce; Council of Economic Advisers.

More specifically, the problem is the falloff from the peak of 1980–1981. But the graph, which has been cast in 1983 dollars by means of the U.S. GNP deflator, shows something else about magnitude: Note the degree to which the ag exports of the 1970s rise above all previous ag imports. In other words, give attention to the timing and size of *record* magnitudes of indicators. And then ask, "Is there anything in the previous historical context of the graph that would have suggested such an extreme record?" In the case of agricultural exports, can you see by examining the graph of 1910 to 1970 that a tripling of the magnitude would soon take place? With your fingers, conceal the 1970s. What "should" have happened next? A continuing rise perhaps, but not a tripling. This, then, is an invitation for inquiry outside the sector being shown.

Let us now go up two steps in aggregate, beyond the national to the international. Figure 9-10 shows the magnitude of world trade in billions of 1973 dollars. The most evident thing about the line is its steady upward growth, with a surge at 1973–1974 and another big change, downward, at 1981–1983. This squares with our previous figure on U.S. agricultural exports, which surged and declined at about the same times as total world trade did. And it makes perfectly good common sense, because one is part of the other. But not all members of the family of items making up world trade will move in sync with the aggregate; for instance, trade in computers did not boom until later than 1973–1974 and did not ease off until after 1981–1983. So aggregate world trade, as a linear trend, should not be expected faithfully to *predict* all its sectors.

We should ask the question once again, "Does the graph itself of Figure 9-10 suggest that there should be the 'big changes' that have obviously happened?" The answer once again is no; the graph indicates that the trend of trade changed, or that it was interrupted, but not why. But the graph also shows *when* the big changes took place, and that will be helpful in an attempt to associate causes. The big change upward in 1973–1974, for instance, is coincident with the OPEC oil embargo; the big change downward in 1981–1983 is coincident with the emergence of record indebtedness by many developing countries.

**Figure 9–10. World trade of all goods has also been through
two big changes recently. Note that labelling the obvious on a
graph can greatly affect one's perception.**

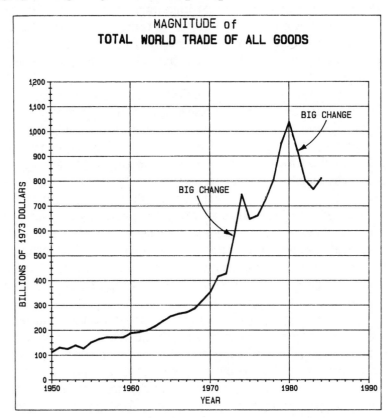

Source: **United Nations, International Monetary Fund.**

On the scale of annual percent change, Figure 9-11 shows that the volatility of world trade is a good candidate for addition to our list of what is meant by the present Age of Uncertainty. In addition to the existence of very high interest rates, we might say that any business dependent on world trade is likely to be more volatile now than at any time since World War II. (Data for world trade before WW II were not reliably kept, so far as I know.)

Let us now turn to the U.S. dollar, picking up once again on my colleague Jim from the research and development department. Figure 9-12 is one that I showed Jim, in an effort to bolster his own insight on the issue of what might happen to the dollar in the future and why no one can predict it. The figure shows the magnitude of the strength of the U.S. dollar in units of "SDRs per dollar." *SDR* means special drawing right; it is the currency of the International Monetary Fund (IMF), and is a specified average of four national currencies—namely, the British pound, the French franc, the German mark, and the Japanese yen. There are other important currencies in the world, but these are the main ones, and the SDR is a good sample for the purpose of trend studies.

As shown in Figure 9-12, the strength of the dollar changed only narrowly for two decades after World War II, after which it took a drop for several years and then a rise. The beginning of the decline, in 1971, is coincident with a change in policy by the Nixon Administration, which removed the dollar from the gold standard and thus abrogated the Bretton Woods monetary agreement of 1944 (implemented in 1947). While the Bretton Woods agreement was in effect, the dollar was stable; after the agreement was broken, the dollar became extremely volatile—as shown in Figure 9-13. The volatility of the dollar must surely be added to our list of items that characterize today's Age of Uncertainty.

But notice Figures 9-14 and 9-15, which illustrate the quarterly and monthly volatility, respectively, of the dollar in the last several years. Quarterly volatility peaked in 1981, monthly volatility in 1978 (with signs of increase in 1985). So if we want to be both accurate and contemporaneous, then the biggest contribution of the dollar to uncertainty is not just its release from a fixed system, but its *continual rise* in the period 1980 to 1985. Now see Figure 9-16. What really surprised people, especially those using econometric models, was the duration and extent of the dollar's rise. This occurred in the face of the U.S. trade deficit, which in theory should have weakened the dollar. (See previous discussion in Chapter 4.)

So we have tested via *quantitative history* the notion that today we face an Age of Uncertainty, in which interest rates have been unusually high, world trade is volatile, the dollar has been both volatile and surprisingly strong, and various sectors of the national economy have been suffering declines of magnitude that appear to be "no fault of their own."

Figure 9–11. World trade of all goods is now at record highs. Thus, when talking about an Age of Uncertainty, we should take into account world trade.

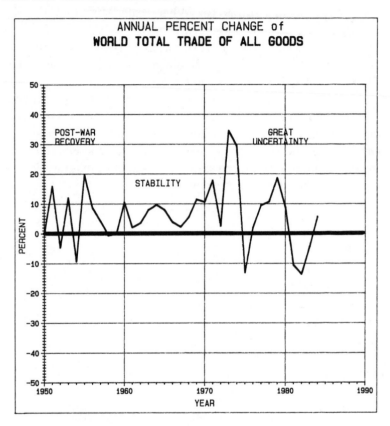

Source: United Nations, International Monetary Fund.

Figure 9–12. The magnitude of the U.S. dollar has changed more in recent times than even world trade has. (Note: *SDR* means special drawing right; it is the currency unit of the International Monetary Fund, or IMF. The SDR is a weighted average of the currencies of Japan, Britain, France, and West Germany.)

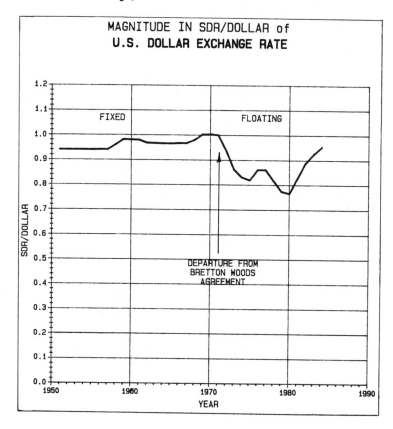

Source: United Nations, International Monetary Fund.

Figure 9–13. The volatility of the U.S. dollar in recent years is also at a record high. The Age of Uncertainty seems much more identifiable with the dollar and world trade, plus high interest rates, than with other economic indicators.

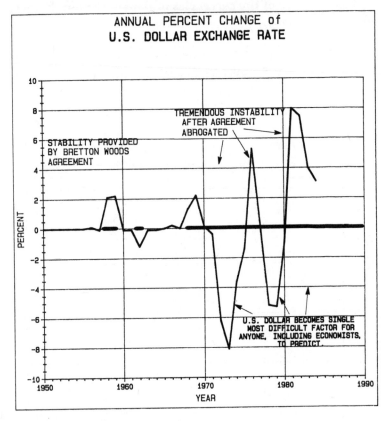

Source: United Nations, International Monetary Fund.

Figure 9-14. The volatility of the dollar, on a quarter-to-quarter basis, peaked in 1979-1980. In the last five years of the "floating exchange rate" system, the volatility has averaged about plus or minus 2 percent.

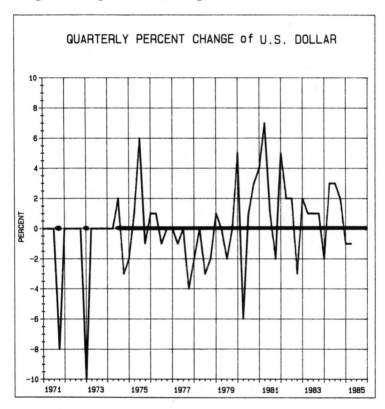

Source: International Monetary Fund, *Financial Statistics.*

Figure 9–15. Like quarterly change, monthly volatility of the dollar peaked in the two-year period of 1978–1980.

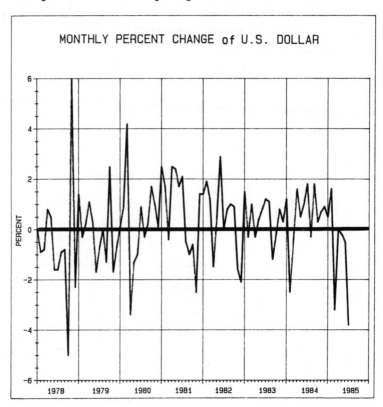

Source: International Monetary Fund, *Financial Statistics.*

Figure 9–16. The big surprise for currency traders in the past few years has not been monthly, or even daily, volatility; it's been the cumulative upward movement of the dollar.

Source: International Monetary Fund, *Financial Statistics.*

Chapter 10

Narrative History

Quantitative history of the type described in the previous chapter is relatively new. The mainstay of scholarship in history is narrative history, which treats a stream of events in a qualitative manner using prose narration. It is rare to find an accomplished narrative historian who draws graphs. But in a very important sense, the graphs are the easy part. Explaining what made the graphs behave as they did, in a manner that enlightens the illative sense, is the hard part.

Let me now repeat from a different perspective my contention about the failure of economists. Economists do not analyze history. Historians do, especially narrative historians. Economists analyze only some of the numerical data associated with history. A better way to handle this data is by straightforward display, not expecting that the data, as if it were independently causal, would of itself regenerate reality. This straightforward display, which I have called quantitative history, can reveal timing and can suggest connections and associations of value to narrative history and to the determining of trends.

QUANTITATIVE VERSUS NARRATIVE HISTORY

To further distinguish between quantitative and narrative, let's take a brief example from a sub-sub-sector of the economy. The sector is agricultural exports again, the sub-sector is grain, and the sub-sub-sector is grain exports using the St. Lawrence Seaway at harvest time. Here are the figures:

Year	Harvest Shipments Oct.–Nov. (in Millions of Bushels)
1980	167
1981	150
1982	113
1983	89
1984	127
1985	55

What happened to the harvest movement of 1985? Why the precipitous drop to 55 million bushels of shipments? (My estimate of data accuracy is plus or minus 5 million bushels in 100 million). Was the dollar so strong that this grain was priced out of the market? One of our previous graphs, Figure 9–16, shows that the dollar was *weakening* in the fall of 1985, not strengthening. And why would only the St. Lawrence Seaway be affected? Here is more context:

Year	St. Lawrence Harvest Shipments (in Millions of Bushels)	Total U.S. Harvest Shipments (in Millions of Bushels)	St. Lawrence Share of U.S. (Percent)
1980	167	931	18
1981	150	966	16
1982	113	805	14
1983	89	846	11
1984	127	909	14
1985	55	680	8

Why did the shipments on the St. Lawrence Seaway fall from an average of 130 million bushels over five years to a record low of 55 million, and to a record low of only 8 percent of the U.S. total? Because a canal broke. From October 13, 1985, to November 6, 1985, the Welland Canal between Lake Erie and Lake Ontario was closed to all shipping, due to the collapse of a wall at Lock Number 7. This explanation is as absolute as you might possibly ever hope to get. Pictures of the broken lock appeared in all newspapers. Eyewitness accounts were reported. Contractors were hired to make repairs. Businesses were directly affected, including my own.

But you could not know this explanation from looking at the shipment data themselves. Numbers are numbers. In a series of figures, no connections are automatically present.

THE ROLE OF VARIABLES IN MODELLING

A future econometrician, however, will not be deterred by the above. The shipment data will be made part, perhaps, of a "regional transportation model," the purpose of which is to forecast the future of various transportation modes on the basis of how, mathematically, the data has interacted in the past. If someone points out to the model's author the facts of the Welland Canal's closing in 1985, the modeller will add a "dummy variable" to the model. The dummy will show "open" for all harvests prior to 1985, and "closed" for 1985 itself. In this way, the mathematical correlations will be preserved, and the modeller can go on with the forecasting. The model will be financed with government funds and used in attempts to induce businesses to locate new operations in this place or that, perhaps on the Seaway.

The term *dummy variable* should be taken literally. Why did the wall of Lock Number 7 collapse? Because it was 54 years old and not properly maintained. Will maintenance charges, and thus tolls on the Seaway, go up? Very probably, yes, they will. And if they do, would you expect the Seaway to then return to servicing its previous share of U.S. grain shipments? You probably wouldn't. So the dummy variable conceals, in favor of mathematical modelling, the real issue—the fact that the Seaway is old and won't keep running for free.

In the foregoing case, the dummy variable might also be called an *Act of God* variable, as if the lock had been struck by a fierce bolt of lightning. Another very popular kind of dummy variable among modellers is the so-called *policy variable,* which is used to strip sets of data of irregularities ("anomalies") thought to have been caused by changes in policy. Whatever interferes with the models is made nameless; this means that political policy becomes an anonymous spoiler to what would otherwise be a smooth running machine. In my view, this is precisely the wrong emphasis to give policy—instead of making it paramount, modellers make it secondary; instead of using it to lead, they make it an interruption.

Although I think it is a somewhat narrow example, the case of the Seaway is instructive. The explanation of record low harvest exports through the Seaway can be given only via narrative history. However, a carefully written account of Lock Number 7 would be of interest, mainly to the several dozen businesses that experienced the direct losses (estimated at a few tens of millions of dollars) in the shutdown.

Let's jump back up to a world-level case involving hundreds of billions of dollars, and explore the role of Narrative History further.

NATIONAL SECURITY AND NARRATIVE HISTORY

Let's take national security. Specifically, let's take the conflict between the United States and the Soviet Union, a deep underlying movement in history that, among other things, has generated hundreds of billions of dollars of business in aircraft, missiles, and other weapons. When did the conflict begin and when will it end? What is your forecast?

I hope you'll agree that it is not unreasonable to request

such a forecast. Many people would say it is the most important question facing mankind today, let alone the future of all aerospace defense industries. I hope also that you will shrink from giving a quick answer, because this question is one of the "big ones" and a mature person who answers it glibly will appear foolish.

And yet what else do we have, in an econometric model of the world economy to the year 2000, but a glib answer to the question I posed on national security, and to many other questions of equal magnitude. A tacit assumption in most if not all such models is that the conflict between the United States and the Soviet Union will continue as is, generating several hundred billions of dollars in economic activity in each country every year. It is not known whether weapons business stimulates or retards the total aggregate of economic activity. A dollar of GNP from an Army tank is accounted for in the same way as a dollar from a Chevrolet.

In the face of the big questions, the questions that rightly humble our illative sense, I recommend a retreat to narrative history. More exactly, I recommend a retreat from the arrogance of economic models to the combined approach of quantitative history backed up by narrative.

ANSWERING THE BIG QUESTIONS

When did the conflict between the United States and the Soviet Union begin? Some would say with the rise of Marx or of Lenin. Some would say before that, inasmuch as the ideas of these two most famous communists and their opposition to capitalism might well have found their way out earlier, in the unheralded resistance of millions of workers before Marx and Lenin were born. So we have to narrow the question, or we will be led far afield.

The way to do this narrowing, in the case of a businessperson, is to think business. When did the conflict between the United States and the Soviet Union begin to affect business?

"Sometime after the Cold War," might be the answer, "because the United States began building nuclear weapons on a production-line basis, along with jet bombers, missiles, and nuclear submarines." When was the Cold War? "Sometime after World War II, because we were officially allies with the Soviets during the war."

Let me hasten this process of narrowing by proposing my own answer, in a method similar to the way that I, a chief researcher, would answer such a question posed by my own chief executive.

I believe that the conflict in question first became evident, at a level that affected business, with the Marshall Plan. The Marshall Plan is frequently cited both in terms of a need, according to America's rulers, to stall Soviet expansionism, and in terms of fostering a recovery of European and Japanese industry that some Americans would one day rue.

In a study of the Marshall Plan, I would begin with timing and magnitude. I would learn that the Marshall Plan cost some $5 billion a year for about three or four years, beginning in 1947. I would wonder how large this was by today's standards, and this would set me to drawing a graph (see Figure 10–1). In this graph, I have chosen to express the magnitudes of annual foreign aid expenditures not in billions of dollars but as a percent of U.S. GNP. This is, I think, simpler and more reliable than using one of the various "deflators" that are available.

The figure shows a large "blip" in the curve of foreign aid between 1947 and 1950, when the values go from 1.0 percent to 2.2 percent before going back down, first to 1.0 percent, then below that, then to its 1984 level of 0.3 percent. I note that 2.2 percent of today's GNP would be enormous:

$$2.2\% \times \$3 \text{ trillion} = \$60 \text{ billion}$$

Even with $200 billion deficits, a new $60 billion foreign aid program would make headlines. What kind of headlines did the Marshall Plan make then, I would wonder. How was it sold to Congress?

Figure 10-1. The Marshall Plan provided a sharp upward "spike" to the downward curve of U.S. foreign aid spending since World War II. The Marshall Plan cost about $5 billion per year, or 2 percent of GNP. That percentage today would amount to over $60 billion.

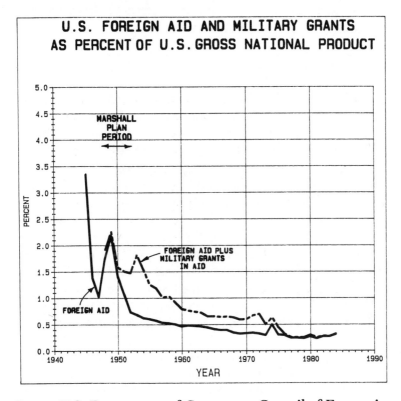

Source: U.S. Department of Commerce; Council of Economic Advisers.

In the book *The Marshall Plan,* Charles L. Mee, Jr. suggests that the plan originated as one thing but was sold as another. It originated as a means of developing markets for American commodities. It was sold as a way to halt the spread of communism in Europe, and it served as a principal means for Truman's election in 1948. The following two anecdotes from the book may shed new light on our analysis of the Cold War.[1]

Markets and the Marshall Plan

William Clayton, then Under Secretary of State for Economic Affairs, was in charge of negotiations with Europe on how big the Marshall Plan should be. Before that, Clayton had been a cofounder of Anderson-Clayton, which still exists today as one of America's largest cotton and soybean companies. I did not know him personally, but I think I know something about this kind of man, who goes from industry to government. If you asked him what was good for America, he would say, "More cotton exports." And what was good for Europe? "More cotton imports." Indeed, to quote Clayton verbatim in 1947, "Let us admit right off that our objective has as its background the needs and interests of the people of the United States. We need markets— big markets—in which to buy and sell."[2] And, further, from a memo of Clayton to Secretary Marshall on May 19, 1947:

> Europe is steadily deteriorating. The political position reflects the economic. . . . Millions of people in the cities are slowly starving. . . . Only until the end of this year can England and France meet the deficits out of their fast-dwindling reserves of gold and dollars. Italy can't go that long. Without further prompt and substantial aid from the United States, economic, social, and political disintegration will overwhelm Europe . . . the immediate effects on our domestic economy would be disastrous: markets for our surplus production gone, unemployment, depression, a heavily unbalanced budget on the background of a mountainous war debt. These things must not happen. Europe must have from us, as a grant, 6 or 7 billion dollars' worth of goods a year for three years.[3]

A New Theory and the Marshall Plan

A junior official in our Moscow embassy in the winter of 1946 was George Kennan, then completely unknown. One day,

> A cable arrived from Washington asking whether the Moscow embassy could explain why the Russians were showing some hesitation about joining the World Bank and the International Monetary Fund. It was a simple question—relayed from the Treasury Department—one that could have been answered easily and without much fanfare, since the Russians simply did not consider it in their interests to join in such arrangements. But Kennan saw the question as an opportunity for him to explain Russia once and for all to the people back in Washington. His superior officer was away, and it fell to him to reply to the request for information. He launched into an 8,000-word cable that constituted a primer of Russian history, and a prospectus of American foreign policy for the next several decades. To his notions of balance-of-power politics, he added a bit of his old hatred of Russia's leaders, a dash of ideological fervor, a lashing of fear, and a call to arms—and casting it all in his fine prose, he gave the folks back home something they could use, something that ravished the insiders back in Washington.[4]

Copies of the cable found their way around Washington. The Secretary of the Navy, James Forrestal, who had just organized the War College in Washington, put in a request to have Kennan "detailed at once to lecture on world affairs to one hundred select military and diplomatic officers." Kennan was good at this. *The New York Times* dubbed him, "America's global planner."[5]

Once again, I did not know Kennan personally, but the story of how his cable struck a need in Washington for a theory (a narrative model) of Soviet behavior, to fill a vacuum, seems entirely plausible. Likewise, the first time something happens, the more powerful its effect; the first time the State Department has a Policy Planning Staff (a "brain trust"), the more powerful it may be.

Kennan's ideas became the key to selling the Marshall Plan.

To Congress, "The argument about European cooperation was awfully abstract and, to most, boring. The argument about building an integrated European market for American goods seemed also to lack fire. The words that were really electrifying up on the Hill were 'Communist threat,' and that was the theme that the salesmen tended to return to again and again as they worked the halls of Congress."[6]

My original question was, "When did the conflict between the United States and the Soviet Union begin, and when will it end? What is your forecast?" I suspect that the two foregoing stories, even in their greatly abbreviated form, may have given you new food for thought. Factual material, in the hands of objective historians, can strike your mind and break up myths. Could it possibly be true that the Soviets didn't start the Cold War—that we did, for the gain of a market, the love of a theory (Kennan's), and the sake of a Presidential election? Maybe, maybe not. That's certainly an irreverent proposition, if ever there were one. But it requires you to read the book from which I quoted, and probably several others. Myths are too strong to be completely shattered by abbreviated passes.

GETTING HELP IN FORECASTING

The central questions on which history and business turn, the deepest underlying trends of all, have little to do with economic indicators, let alone with their mathematical manipulation. To tune in on this wavelength, you must break through the commonly held myths. To forecast the major trends, your mind needs factual narrative on the broadest possible outlines of history. Irreverent denial of myths of the past will teach you to detect new ones about the future, sooner than your competition.

In a pursuit of a goal of this magnitude, you must have help. Although you need to trust yourself to sniff out the topics that will matter, after that you need help in choosing what to read. The library of research on such a topic as this is absolutely enormous. There are tens of thousands of books on just the subject of United States–Soviet relations. If you are an executive in a large corporation, the kind of experts you need as assistants, and the role for your chief researcher, change.

If you are not part of a large organization—let's say you are both your own chief executive and chief researcher—you still need help. Whatever resources you devote to acquiring outside expertise need to be redirected. If you follow the recommendations in this book, you will find yourself much more frequently in the humanities; and within the humanities, experts will be plenteous, though at first rather surprised that you're asking.

Chapter 11

Critical History

The first branch of history examined here was quantitative, the second narrative. Quantitative history deals primarily with the display of indicators; we look for timing and association, but don't *expect* that a causal model will emerge. Narrative history deals with the qualitative facts of history, cast in the form of written stories; we rely on professional historians to dig through old memoranda and records and to write objective accounts of what happened; we judge the plausibility of the resulting stories according to our own experience in similar matters.

In both of these branches of history, the businessperson needs expert assistance, from his researcher and from others. He needs help in choosing from among the millions available, which books and articles to read, after he has indicated his own interests and the location of his "frontier of knowledge." He needs help also in the presentation of quantitative data—the actual drawing of graphs—because the high quality display of data in graphs usually requires a more specialized skill with computers than is necessary for the executive to acquire.

(I will use the pair of "executive and researcher" as my principle audience. Most readers will be closer to one of these roles than the other, but some readers will be in both simultaneously—that is, they will be both executive of their affairs and researcher of whatever they feel needs researching. This latter group will have an easier job of applying my recommendations, for only the attitude of a single mind needs to be changed. In the case of a large corporation, however, not only must the executive's attitude be changed, but so must the researcher's—and both must still confront the corporate culture as rebels, or converts to an unusual approach. So, as a rhetorical device, I will focus on the audience with the hardest task, and assume that others will translate for themselves.)

As we approach the third branch of history, *critical history,* we are giving notice to all experts and all helpers that the executive is directly involved in the process, and is in fact responsible for its authenticity. If the executive is not willing to take a hands-on approach to critical history, then the benefits promised by the entire approach in this book will be considerably lessened.

The old name for critical history is *philology,* which to medieval scholars meant "the comparison of texts." How does one know that the data presented are really the data they are said to be? What changes have been made in the data as they are passed from originator to typesetter to first user, to critic, to interpreter, and so on down the line? How can one be sure that the information is in its rawest form, with no causal connections added by other people?

A present-day business leader interested in U.S. housing starts should be sure to have the latest raw figures, as a first step, before accepting someone's interpretation of what the figures mean. Otherwise he or she will never be able to get disentangled from the econometric models into which housing figures are immediately put by most experts. Business leaders must try to deal directly with the figures in their own mind, without help, or with no more than clerical help, or else they will miss their best chance of beating their competition—through their own ability to forecast trends better than any economic model can possibly do.

The exercise I'm about to recommend with respect to economic data is similar to starting up an accounting system. Suppose you sat down with a clean sheet of paper and began to list what you wanted your controller to send you in the way of company performance data. You know what you want—a better and more immediate grasp of operational realities—and you know how it should look when it's done. Executives can and should exercise the same prerogative with their researchers. They should make a list of what they want to know about the economy and how the report should look when it's done properly.

Here's how to do it. Ask yourself, "What are the economic factors of most interest to me?" In posing the question, try to separate what you've been told by others to be interested in from what you yourself *are* interested in. "What stories in the paper catch my eye, time after time?" There will be a reason for this— your mind is looking for the things it needs to do its job, regardless of what your experts have been saying.

In making your list, remember that you are not trying to be complete, the way an economist would mean "complete." You are not an empirical scientist attempting to capture the entire universe of published economic data, and then be able to solve for the correct answer. This can't be done anyway. There is no correct answer. It is *okay* to ignore factors that others seem to talk about a lot, providing that your honest appraisal is that those things have never helped you or interested you in the past.

What you are trying to do here is make yourself a tiny bit better than you already are, at what you already do well. You are attempting to set things up to enable yourself to display your opinions and ideas, in the hope of finding errors, myths, omissions, contradictions, and areas for more careful study—all of which will push out your frontiers.

Ask yourself the question once again, "What are the economic factors of most interest to *me*?" Without consulting any text or asking anyone, make a list. Don't worry about exact names if you don't know them. Use slang for what you remember.

The next step is to go to the library and get the current issue of *Economic Indicators,* a monthly publication. This 35-page document is prepared by the Council of Economic Advisers for the Joint Economic Committee of Congress and is printed by the Government Printing Office. It contains almost exclusively numbers, with a few graphs, but has no interpretive text. It is meant to be a handy collection of the economic data that members of

Congress and bureaucrats most often want. It is by no means complete, not even at the national level, and especially not at the regional or international level.

Flip through *Economic Indicators* and examine the table of contents. Try, without help, to find the items on your list. If it turns out that an indicator you want to follow is not in this publication, be aware that most other people, especially members of Congress (who affect your business mightily), are therefore probably not following it. If one of your items isn't present, it is most likely (1) regional (state or city), (2) international, which Congress is weak at following, or (3) industry-specific, beyond the major categories of automobiles, steel, and housing. The process of critical history that you apply to regional, international, and industry-specific data is identical to what you should do when dealing with the national economy, except you'll use publications other than *Economic Indicators*. So let me continue with the example at the national level.

Let's go back to the list of economic factors of personal interest to you, and let's assume now that you have put aside those other than the ones dealing with the national economy. How long is the list? How long should it be? Let me be ridiculous at one extreme: If you listed 100 things, that's too many. You're kidding yourself. I won't deny that the mind can handle a hundred things at once, but you won't be able to *track* that many in a data base without turning the job over to a computer model. The idea here is to *not* turn the job over. The idea is to do what's practical with data to improve your own mind, especially to bolster your skepticism, your ability to tell myth from fact. It wouldn't be practical to keep track of 100 factors.

At the other extreme, if your list had only two or three items, it's too short. I would grant you that most market decisions will hinge on mainly a couple of items, but this is usually after extensive debate has substantially narrowed down the starting list to the two or three things that are the hardest to determine.

As a starting point, I recommend a list that is "several" items long. To me, several is "seven plus or minus two." Eventually your new data base might have the following:

1. Five to nine indicators on the national economy.
2. Five to nine indicators on the international economy.
3. Five to nine regional indicators.
4. Five to nine industry-specific indicators.

If you are managing a business with many divisions and many locations, then there may be more than a total of four sets of data, but I recommend erring on the side of too small rather than too big. It may be more appropriate for divisional or regional managers to set up and maintain the data than for the executive at headquarters to do it.

Back now to *Economic Indicators*. Set aside a couple of hours on a Saturday. Buy a data pad like that shown in Figure 11–1. The number of years to display and the sequence in which to put the indicators on your list is very, very important. In making the table for yourself, you are communicating to yourself what you really believe about how things work, and how you can best follow events as they unfold and test your views. For instance, if you believe that interest rates cause everything, and GNP is a result, put interest rates in column 1, GNP in column 7. Or if you think that the deficit is of primary importance, put it in column 1, and perhaps put interest rates next to it. If you think it all starts with the confidence of people to produce, put GNP in column 1.

Arrange your factors on the national economy in some kind of order, even if it's somewhat arbitrary. You can change the order later. In fact, this is the key point: In the ever-evolving complexity of man's affairs, some factors will come to the fore, others will recede. Your job is to be better than your competition at judging what's in column 1 today.

Let's say you have a data pad that looks like Figure 11–2. You have not only selected a list of indicators, but you have also put them into a tentative order—and you have said, "I'm going to look several years back, at least to begin with."

Figure 11–1. Find a data pad with about eight columns—one for years, the others for economic indicators.

BLANK DATA PAD

Figure 11–2. Fill in the range of years that you feel is needed
to provide a good sense of history, and fill in the names of the
indicators that interest you most. The order of indicators is
important: Start at the upper left with the most major ones,
and move across the right toward the ones with the most
impact on your particular business.

SELECTION OF YEARS AND INDICATORS

	U.S. MRCH TRADE BAL	U.S. GNP 1972$	U.S. BDGT DFCT	FED MONEY SPLY M-1	CNSMR PRICE INDX	NEW HOME MRTG YIELD	NEW HOUSE STARTS
CAL YEAR	BIL$	PERCNT CHANGE	BIL$	PERCNT CHANGE	PERCNT CHANGE	PERCNT	THSNDS
1976							
1977							
1978							
1979							
1980							
1981							
1982							
1983							
1984							
1985							

The next task is to write in the numbers. This won't be as easy as it sounds. It is here that you will come up against the core of critical history, and its value for you. For the indicators on your list, which you may have expressed in general terms, you will now have to get specific, and you will have to choose between an indicator's *total* and its *parts*, between its *base* and its *change*, and between its *unadjusted* and *adjusted* form. In most cases, however, you will be able to find the form of the indicator that has been of interest to you in news stories. For instance, in GNP it is usually *total* and *change*; that is, U.S. total GNP grew at 6.8 percent in 1985, adjusted to 1972 dollars. In housing starts, it is *total* and *base*; that is, total U.S. housing starts were 1,800 thousand in 1985, seasonally adjusted. In prime interest rate, it is *total* and *base*; that is, prime interest in 1985 was 10.2 percent as an unadjusted average.

At this point you will probably also become aware that annual figures are not enough to meet the pace of how often things in the economy change; you will want quarterly and in some cases monthly data. But for the moment, stick with annual figures.

Your data pad should now look like Figure 11–3, and you are ready to have a discussion with your researcher. If you've never designed such a data base, your researcher will certainly be impressed. He or she will see that you are serious and that you are willing to study the data in its raw form. Tell your researcher that you're providing a rough form of how you believe you could best follow the national economy; that you want the researcher to clean it up and add months and quarters; that you want to develop similar tables for international, regional, and industry-specific factors; and that you want the researcher to maintain them for you and give you regular updates. If all goes well, the researcher would supply you with a table such as that shown in Figure 11–4.

Once you start receiving clean versions of your own list of economic indicators, what do you do? What's the purpose of the whole exercise? You put down in your own hand, at the bottom of the table, your own forecasts of the future. You do this every time you get an updated table. Before you make a fresh forecast, however, you score how well you did on the last one. You check your projected figures against what the numbers actually became, when released by the government. When you are wrong, you challenge your own arguments. Maybe you need to change the order of your factors, or maybe you are missing some factors that have now made themselves felt.

To whom does your copy of the table go, with your own forecast? My recommendation is to no one. In its details, it is between you and you. Whatever business decisions you are making in any given period of time will be affected, willy-nilly, by your forecast of the future, whether or not you have the kind of indicator tables I recommend. In other words, no business person is ever without a forecast. But very few of your competitors, even if a book like this were in wide circulation, will go to the effort to make their own forecasts visible to themselves, to enable their minds to improve.

Figure 11–3. Complete your database by using entries from *Economic Indicators* (or other sources). Use the same units and decimal places that your source does, for easy comparison when revisions are made.

COMPLETED DATA BASE

	U.S. MRCH TRADE BAL	U.S. GNP 1972$	U.S. BDGT DFCT	FED MONEY SPLY M-1	CNSMR PRICE INDX	NEW HOME MRTG YIELD	NEW HOUSE STARTS
CAL YEAR	BIL$	PERCNT CHANGE	BIL$	PERCNT CHANGE	PERCNT CHANGE	PERCNT	THSNDS
1976	-9.5	5.4	-73.7	6.0	4.8	8.99	1538
1977	-31.1	5.5	-53.6	8.1	6.8	9.01	1987
1978	-33.9	5.0	-59.0	8.3	9.0	9.54	2020
1979	-27.5	2.8	-40.2	7.2	13.3	10.78	1745
1980	-25.5	-0.3	-73.8	6.6	12.4	12.66	1292
1981	-28.0	2.5	-78.9	6.5	8.9	14.70	1084
1982	-36.4	-2.1	-127.9	8.8	3.9	15.14	1062
1983	-62.0	3.7	-207.8	9.8	3.8	12.57	1703
1984	-108.3	6.8	-185.3	5.8	4.0	12.38	1749
1985			-211.3				

Figure 11–4. Completed database from researcher to executive. Researcher adds quarters and months and issues updates using new government figures. Executive pencils in forecasts and then compares those insights with actual figures.

DATA BASE AUGMENTED BY RESEARCHER

H-25 CRTHSTRY .WKS	CAL YEAR	1 U.S. MRCH TRADE BALANCE BIL$	2 U.S. GNP PERCENT CHANGE 1972$	3 FEDERAL BUDGET DEFICT BIL$	4 FED MONEY SUPPLY M-1 PERCENT CHANGE	5 CNSMR PRICE INDEX PERCENT CHANGE	6 NEW HOME MRTG YIELD PERCENT	7 NEW HOUSE STARTS THSNDS
(P.) is page in Economic Indicators		(P.36)	(P.3)	(P.32)	(P.26)	(P.24)	(P.30)	(P.19)
	1976	-9.5	5.4	-73.7	6	4.8	8.99	1538
	1977	-31.1	5.5	-53.6	8.1	6.8	9.01	1987
	1978	-33.9	5.0	-59.0	8.3	9.0	9.54	2020
	1979	-27.5	2.8	-40.2	7.2	10.78	10.78	1745
	1980	-25.5	-0.3	-73.8	6.6	12.4	12.66	1292
	1981	-28.0	2.5	-78.9	6.5	8.9	14.70	1084
	1982	-36.4	-2.1	-127.9	8.8	3.9	15.14	1062
	1983	-62.0	3.7	-207.8	9.8	3.8	12.57	1703
	1984	-108.3	6.8	-185.3	5.8	4.0	12.38	1749
FORECAST	1985			-211.3				
		SEASNLY ADJ	SEASNLY ADJ ANNUAL		SEASNLY ADJ 6-MNTH	MONTH TO MONTH	MONTHLY	SEASNLY ADJ ANNUAL
	JAN				5.9	0.2	12.27	1849
	FEB				7.6	0.3	12.21	1647
	MAR				7.6	0.5	11.92	1889
85-I		-29.5	0.3		7.0	0.3	12.13	1795
	APR				9.9	0.4	12.05	1933
	MAY				10.3	0.2	12.01	1681
	JUN				12.1	0.2	11.75	1701
85-II		-33.0	1.9		10.8	0.3	11.94	1772
	JUL				12.1	0.2	11.34	1647
	AUG				13.3	0.2	11.24	1749
	SEP							
85-III			2.8		12.7	0.2	11.29	1698
	OCT							
	NOV							
	DEC							
FORECAST 85-IV								

Chapter 12

Graphic Distortion

The delineation of trends requires using graphs, and the methods of graphing are usually taught under the heading of "Cartesian Coordinates" in high school geometry. After that, formal education in the matter stops—even Ph.D. programs in which graphing is central, such as economics, offer no special training in how to construct good graphs. There are proper ways to graph trends, and there are ways in which graphs may be used to illustrate trends that are not present and to grossly exaggerate ones that are.

An example of a properly prepared graph is shown in Figure 12-1. The subject matter is United States new housing starts, and the issue is whether the trend is on an upswing or a downswing. The time frame is 24 months. To prepare a "proper" graph like the one in Figure 12-1, follow these rules:

1. Use *line* graphs, not bar graphs or other types.
2. Use axes of approximately equal length to result in a *square,* not rectangular, grid.
3. Begin the *y*-axis at zero, *always,* when displaying the magnitude of an indicator.
4. Extend the *y*-axis far enough so that the trendline itself is approximately centered in the coordinate field.
5. Extend the *x*-axis well beyond the final data point.
6. Always plot gridlines, both horizontal and vertical ones. Size the grid so that there are ten gridlines (plus or minus two), both horizontally and vertically.

Figure 12–1. This shows the "proper" way to graph 18 months of housing starts. The y-axis starts at zero, the trendline is positioned in the middle of a square grid, and the x-axis extends beyond the final data point.

Source: Economic Indicators (Council of Economic Advisers).

The conclusion I would draw from looking at the graph in Figure 12-1 is that housing starts are relatively stable; perhaps, but not certainly, they bottomed out in October 1984. If I wanted to illustrate this conclusion more forcefully, and I didn't care about objectivity, I would graph it as shown in Figure 12-2. In flattening out the square frame, I have flattened the trendline itself. Rectangular graphs do this whether you want it done or not.

Someone who disagrees with my conclusion of stability in housing starts could provide Figure 12-3. By chopping off the *y*-axis and not showing its zero-point, the *changes* are emphasized—and a downwardness over all 18 months is also introduced.

A bar chart with *y*-axis and *x*-axis foreshortened emphasizes volatility, as demonstrated in Figure 12-4. Figure 12-5 uses vertical rectangularity of the graph's framework to emphasize upwardness.

Changing a graph's framework literally changes the framework of the analysis. A person who chops off the *y*-axis so that small changes are easier to see harbors a belief that small changes make a difference. Maybe they do, but maybe they don't.

When you see a graph that violates the rules of objective graphing, the graph's author may have deliberately distorted the material or may have done so accidentally. Generally speaking, those who draw graphs so that you are forced to focus on change instead of magnitude believe in the econometric approach. Their models depend on tiny changes in the indicators, fed through multiple-correlation equations. It will not seem "dishonest" to them to show you graphs that are "distorting the truth."

If you believe that change is indeed more important than magnitude, then I recommend a graphing procedure that clearly identifies your approach. Figure 12-6 illustrates this method. For the time period of interest—which must be chosen by the analyst, as it won't be chosen automatically by the data—calculate the average (or the slope of the trend, if it's clearly present). Then express each monthly figure in terms of a deviation from that average. For instance, in the case of our present example, the average monthly number of housing starts is 1,765. For August 1985, the figure is 1,749. August is thus 1,765 − 1,749 = 16 units below average. In percent deviation from average this is (16 × 100) ÷ 1,765 = 1 percent. This calculation is made for each month, resulting in the graph shown in Figure 12-6.

Now suppose that you suspect that changes in housing starts are affected by changes in home mortgage interest rates. You find a monthly indicator for mortgage rates, calculate the percent deviation from the average over the same period used for housing starts, and display the two lines as shown in Figure 12-7.

What can be concluded from Figure 12-7? (1) Upward changes in mortgage rates tend to be associated with downward changes in housing starts, but with notable exceptions. (2) Housing starts in May, June, and July of 1985 were down from the average despite lower mortgage rates. Were loan standards changed? Did prospective housing buyers spend money on something else? Was disposable income less?

The value of Figure 12-7 is that you can see the extent of reliability in the common assertion that as interest rates fall, housing starts increase. "All other things being equal," an economist might say. If, however, the same economist went on to model all the other factors that affect housing, and then proceeded to say that a particular one had a particular effect, I would certainly disagree.

Mathematics and graphing will not allow you to harness the universe. No variables are truly independent. You cannot make "all other things equal." You can only recast one problem in terms of another.

But seeing an old problem in a new fresh way is often worth lots of money to us, especially if we see it before our competitors do.

One final caveat about Figure 12-7. The base of housing numbers is four digits (for example, 1,765; 1,820; and so on), whereas the base of mortgage rates is only two digits (12.5 percent, 11.9 percent, and so on). When this disparity in bases is present, there will often be a disparity in the percent change as well. But this should not be taken to mean that one indicator is either more or less volatile than the other. The reason is in the nature of percentages themselves: When I am 1 year old and become 2, my age is 100 percent greater; yet when I am 10 years old and become 11, my age is only 10 percent greater. The size of the base affects the calculation of percentages, and it cannot be escaped in the presentation of results. Presentation is of equal importance to analysis. Graphic distortion costs society perhaps billions of dollars every year.

Figure 12–2. This is an improper graph. Flattening the square grid into a rectangle also flattens the trendline, making the slope difficult to determine.

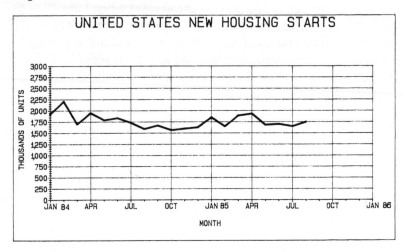

Source: Economic Indicators (Council of Economic Advisers).

Figure 12–3. **In this improper graph, the *y*-axis does not start at zero, which exaggerates the variability of the data.**

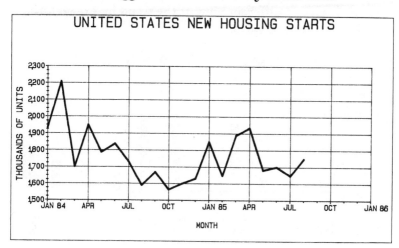

Source: Economic Indicators (Council of Economic Advisers).

Figure 12–4. This improper graph is a bar chart in which the
y-axis is foreshortened and the x-axis is clipped of several
months; it gives a different view of the trend by exaggerating
month-to-month increases.

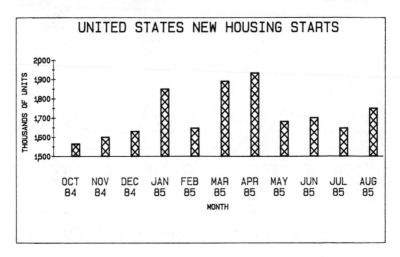

Source: Economic Indicators (Council of Economic Advisers).

Figure 12-5. This improper chart squeezes the data into a vertical rectangle, which introduces an upward bias to the trend that was not apparent in another view of the same data (see Figure 12-4).

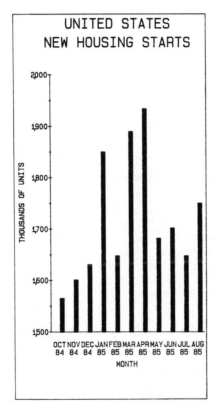

Source: Economic Indicators (Council of Economic Advisers).

Figure 12–6. The proper way to display *changes* in monthly data is as a percent deviation from the average.

Source: Economic Indicators (Council of Economic Advisers).

Figure 12-7. This shows the proper way to display changes in order to see whether two factors are correlated. In this case, upward moves of mortgage rates are often, but not always, associated with downward moves in housing starts.

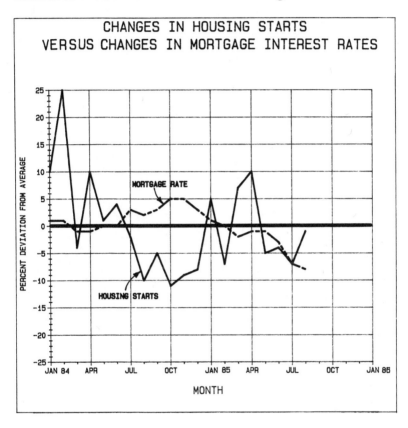

Source: Economic Indicators (Council of Economic Advisers).

Chapter 13

Clarity versus Jargon

The businessperson who has taken me seriously so far will have gone to the researcher to ask for three things:

1. Assistance in choosing history books and articles.
2. Assistance in constructing and maintaining data bases on aspects of the economy tailored to the executive's personal interests.
3. Provision of graphs without distortions.

This will be shock enough, no doubt, especially if the researcher started out as an economist. But the present chapter deals with an even more important request than all three of the above, namely:

4. Clarity at all times, both spoken and written, *with no jargon.*

The language of business, in its written form, has come under enormous, mostly well-deserved, criticism in recent years. A full catalog of the alleged weaknesses—running from obscurity to pomposity—requires a lengthy lecture, and that is not my intent here. I want to address just one aspect of the problem, namely jargon, and I want to approach the subject first from a positive point of view. The good that jargon brings to business is often ignored by those giving the lectures.

The more efficient a business has become, I would argue, the more likely you are to find practitioners using lots of jargon. *Jargon* means the specialized or technical language of a trade or profession, or of a particular company. If a commodities broker says, "Sell ten Dec. corn," the order-taker at the other end of the phone, perhaps on the floor of an exchange, knows exactly what to do. The two people can skip all the extra verbiage and use an agreed-upon code. It is efficient. Whenever business is faced with routine operations that are specialized and repetitive, jargon is invented automatically. It saves time and money.

But suppose the head commodities trader says to the chief executive, "We should dump out of this business—with the Fed pulling in and the dollar up, foreign economies will stay in the tank, loan rates will go down, our cash basis will stay narrow, and Chicago May–Dec. will never widen out. We can't make any money." The chief executive, if he came up through the ranks of traders, may believe he knows approximately what the head trader means, but in my opinion he should reject this kind of argument as no argument at all. In other words, jargon, useful as it is in making daily operations efficient, should have as little role in strategic thinking as possible.

Strategic thinking is the most important function of the chief executive. Strategic thinking is the matching of assets with trends. The executive searches for the intersection of his company's abilities with his ideas about the future. The exercise is a time to be as free as possible from any kind of nonsense. It is a time to insist on clear, simple, plain language—and full context. No shortcuts. And at the same time, no elaborate pomposity.

Many textbooks of business prescribe a "special language" for strategic thinking—with precise, special meanings suggested for such terms as *objectives, tactics, strengths and weaknesses,* and *strategies.* I believe that there can be no recipe for clear thinking, there can be only clear thinking. You cannot use a checklist to obtain easy results; you've got to invest the outright hard work of summoning up intellectual honesty (to the degree you have it) and applying it to the business operations of interest. The best recipe is a clean tablet. The best outcome is a statement in plain

English—no buzz words. When it comes to strategic thinking, jargon obscures meaning, because jargon is stripped from the context you need to match internal operations with the external trends that will in the long run dominate profits. Achieving clear language in business planning does not require an elaborate manual, it simply requires a dedicated desire for it by the chief executive. People are capable of speaking and writing in clear prose if they are pushed to do so. The thrust is akin to the preceding chapters: If the leader adopts a new bearing in a need for assistance, there will emerge a group of assistants who find out how to provide what the executive needs. Those who are not accustomed to talking and writing in plain English, and certainly economists are frequently among such a group, will, when the executive consistently demands clarity instead of jargon, learn how to conform. Every community that has a major business will also have major resources in the humanities; local colleges and universities can be tapped for "midnight instruction," if need be, on how to write clearly—at a very low cost compared with the payback that clarity provides to business strategy.

Here is my central thesis: If you cannot explain something in simple language, you may not understand it yourself and other people will have difficulty understanding you. More money is made, more competitors are beaten, when all pretenses are dropped. Complexity of language is a clue that no one clearly understands the situation. Business situations, to be made profitable, must be grasped by a single mind, that of the chief executive. Grasp is increased as language is made simple, as context is expressed in plain words from ordinary speech. Jargon must be banished from strategic thinking. Irreverence and skepticism should penetrate myths, so that underlying trends are as clear as they can be. You must rely on yourself, not on experts with models, to apprehend trends. Help is needed, but of a different kind than economists have been giving.

Chapter 14

Monitoring the Front Page

In the present age, very little stays secret for long. Trends, even in their infancy, are reported on the front page. The difficulty is distinguishing the genuine from the myth, and in disentangling one's own desires for the future from what the future is most likely to be.

By *front page* I mean literally the front page of a single issue of a single paper. But I also mean the entire newspaper; I'm talking about the collective body of information unleashed on civilization every day by thousands of printing presses in hundreds of countries. It is better for the executive to be content with what's on the front page than to yearn for all the details from all the pages in the universe of information. In an important sense, then, I am in disagreement with John Naisbitt, author of *Megatrends,* who apparently has dozens of readers concentrating on hundreds of small-town newspapers, looking for new details. I would claim that what they find are new ideas rather than megatrends. But I would hasten to add that the new ideas are often quite interesting. Furthermore, the disagreement is easily solved: If you believe, according to the way that your own mind works, that Naisbitt's findings are important, simply add him to your own "front page."

The front page is what you make it; it is what you believe contains coverage of the things of greatest importance to the broadest number of people, and thus eventually to business. Political events, at home and abroad, deserve the most prominent place in your front page. Politics is superior to economics; political ideas and conflicts, as we discussed in the case of the United States versus the Soviet Union, will produce the main trends of interest to business.

Technology could itself be called a trend, but I am setting aside technology somewhat from the present discussion. What you do to follow technology is different from what you do to follow the *market* for technology. I am concerned with the market. Following the emergence of new technology for its technical essence requires a different method of monitoring—centering on research and development efforts, scanning the scientific literature, participating in government grants, attending scientific symposia, sponsoring university efforts, and so on.

POLITICAL AND CULTURAL TRENDS

With this in mind, let's return to the political and cultural trends that will be the fabric for the markets of the future, whether involving old technology or new. The British writer George Orwell, who wrote *1984,* had this to say about monitoring:

> To see what is in front of one's nose needs a constant struggle. One thing that helps toward it is to keep a diary, or, at any rate, to keep some kind of record of one's opinions about important events. Otherwise, when some particularly absurd belief is exploded by events, one may simply forget that one ever held it. Political predictions are usually wrong, but even when one makes a correct one, to discover *why* one was right can be very illuminating. In general, one is only right when either wish or fear coincides with reality. If one recognizes this, one cannot, of course, get rid of one's subjective feelings, but one can to some extent insulate them from one's thinking and make predictions cold-bloodedly, by the book of arithmetic.[1]

In the previous chapter on critical history, I proposed that executives put their own forecasts of the main indicators in pencil at the bottom of their monthly updates, and that they take time to assess their mistakes each month. This is a diary. This is the core of what is meant by "monitoring." As Orwell suggests, however, the concept can be widened easily to include qualitative as well as the quantitative elements. A notebook of clippings containing your own assessment of the front page of politics can be enormously useful, especially if you assign probabilities (Orwell's "book of arithmetic"). Look back over it periodically and give yourself an honest grade on how well you did forecasting trends.

You will fail when you confuse what you want to happen from what *is* happening. This very human tendency is a special problem for executives, because most will occasionally have to wear the hat of lobbyist as well as that of forecaster. A clear separation must be made. Nothing will decrease profits faster than aiming your assets at a trend you *want* rather than at one that *is*.

The key feature of monitoring the front page is seeing what is. If something is a myth, it should be so labelled. Much of what is on the front page is indeed myth. But people believe myths, so they play a massive role in the emergence of trends. The act of labelling a myth properly (which requires skepticism and irreverence) improves your ability to estimate its eventual impact—and your ability to separate your own lobbying from your own forecasting.

Much of what appears on the front page about economics comes from experts who, whether they realize it or not, present a view of the way things should work in a free market. This, of course, ignores the reality of governments and politics. ("If things were as we would wish, then we would have our wishes.") In the fall of 1985, I attended a conference that was addressed by the Under Secretary of Agriculture. During the question-and-answer period, an economist chided the Under Secretary for not putting more stress on the over-valued dollar. The Under Secretary replied that the dollar was higher than we in agriculture would prefer it but that the dollar reflects economic reality. The questioner, undaunted, launched into a description of PPP (purchasing power parity), which he said we could use to calculate with certainty, that the dollar is 30 percent over-valued. The Under Secretary shrugged and made no further comment. To me, and I think to the Under Secretary as well, that economist is simply missing what was on the front page. Reality is not obliged to conform with PPP theory, or any other theory. Neither are public officials.

The linguistic markers of theory and myth are euphemism and rhetoric. *Euphemism* is the substitution of an inoffensive term for one considered offensively explicit. For instance, instead of a White House press release saying, "A thousand men, women, and children were bombed with napalm," we might see, "A village was pacified." In a famous essay written in 1946 called "Politics and the English Language," George Orwell said:

> In our time, political speech and writing are largely the defense of the indefensible. Things like the continuance of British rule in India, the Russian purges and deportations, the dropping of the atom bombs on Japan, can indeed be defended, but only by arguments which are too brutal for most people to face, and which do not square with the professed aims of political parties. Thus political language has to consist largely of euphemism, question-begging and sheer cloudy vagueness.[2]

Orwell was reacting to his experience under BBC censors during the war, but his characterization of political language stands.

Rhetoric, as I am using the phrase, is unsupported or inflated discourse that usually attempts to make an emotional impact. For instance, someone who claims that the dollar is "over-valued" has an ax to grind; someone who says we have "under-invested" in high technology has a different kind of ax. And the person who appeals to "parity" is using a general concept to conceal a private formula that will perforce omit the factors that make reality reality. The Bipartisan Budget Appeal discussed in Chapter 8 is a good example of rhetoric.

Politics as reported on the front page will have lots of euphemism and rhetoric, and business reporting uses lots of economic jargon. Here's an example of the latter, taken from a *New York Times* article of October 14, 1985, called, "Economy Gives Alternating Signals": "The economy rebounded smartly during the third quarter, and there are no signs that the nearly four-year expansion is about to expire, statistics to be published this week are expected to show."[3] As you can see, it's not enough to speculate on what all the numbers mean *after* they are published, we must do it beforehand. Once you have your own economic indicators coming to you in the form you want, are updating them routinely using officially released data, are making your own explicit forecasts, and are criticizing the forecasts' accuracy, you should *skip* articles such as the one above. In fact, you should skip nearly all interpretive articles. Stop reading them the moment you find economic jargon, unless the author, perhaps, is someone you regularly follow and respect, or unless you are venturing into a new area and simply need to develop context before you trust yourself.

Political news stories, with or without euphemism and rhetoric, deserve to be read, and read carefully. I often read the President's speeches until I think I know where he stands on issues of importance to my business, and I test my grasp by writing down what I believe he thinks, in plain English. I do the same when new pieces of legislation are introduced, until I grasp their structure; I don't follow every day's drama in Congress, usually, because the characters are too numerous. I mark clippings as I read, and label things as I see them—especially myths, rhetoric, and jargon.

As mentioned previously, the front page is what we choose to make it. It goes beyond *The New York Times* or whatever your main paper is. Your own front page is what you choose to make it, and it should have components from not only daily publications, but from weekly, monthly, quarterly, and beyond. Weekly magazines such as *Time* and *Business Week* attempt to cover the principal trends affecting the consumer and business in a way that daily newspapers can't. The same can be said of monthlies and quarterlies, especially in regard to scholarly publications. It is a good idea to have a few of these on your reading list, if only to illustrate the difference between what comes from the system of "peer review" and what comes from drama-driven journalists.

PERSONAL EXPERIENCE

Another part of the front page is your own attendance at various conferences and symposia. It may be that live gatherings are second only to newspapers for impact on us, and for the instilling of new ideas. Executives who attend out-of-town conferences get away from their routines; they have "climbed from their trenches," and they have tacitly agreed to open themselves up to fresh new ideas. The conference organizers have gathered the best speakers they can find, the ones noted for stirring audiences. Even if the speaker is a scholar with hundreds of articles published, the peer-review process renders that person much "grander" at a conference than in scholarly writing. The scholar thinks, "I've got to liven it up for the audience," and knows that no one is going to review the material before the speech. Thus the live conference has a way of becoming more of a political platform, for economists and others, than anything else on your front page. Keep this in mind as you take notes and later repeat to colleagues what you learned.

INFORMATION OVERLOAD

Much of what's on the front page will be followed by your competitors as well as by you. In other words, the bulk of news has to be followed in a defensive manner. If you don't know about a new development and they do, you're at a disadvantage. This is another way of saying that we live in an age of information overload, and that there is a minimum amount we must absorb to be viable. This does not mean, however, that we should try for maximum saturation. That would take us all the way back to intercepting *every* indicator that rolls off the government presses, which would require turning the intellectual process over to a team of people running a mathematical model. As I've said, such models will not produce as accurate a forecast as you can yourself, by means of a talented selection of what you read and a deliberate policy of what to exclude.

A cartoon in *The New Yorker* in June of 1985 showed a man in an easy chair watching television; on the screen was an announcer, using a pointer to show the four digit number, "2407." The caption read, "Today's number is two thousand four hundred and seven. That's sixteen above normal for this date and thirty-eight ahead of last month at this time." We hear so many numbers, we simply cannot know what they all mean—so there might as well be a number given that's just a number. Someone will find something to which it correlates nicely.

The point is more than media overload. I have said earlier that the universe is complex, more complex than we think it is, more than we can imagine it to be. It has been this way always, even before the media blitz of the twentieth century. Life ceases if we don't simplify. And when following numbers we *must* simplify—carefully, but definitely.

Another article in *The Times*, "Take Your Eye Off the Ball, Scientist Coaches Sluggers" is also of interest. According to Professor A. Terry Bahill of the University of Arizona's Industrial Engineering Department, "The big league fastball simply moves too fast for the eye to follow. By trying to keep his eye on the ball, even a keen-eyed batter will lose sight of it by the time it gets within five feet of the plate." Bahill says, "If a batter is to become a better hitter, he must train himself to occasionally take his eye off the ball in the middle of its trajectory, then voluntarily shift his field of vision closer to home plate and wait for the ball to arrive in that area."[4] This is analogous to what I recommend about monitoring economic indicators and the front page of trends. You need to implement deliberate systems, but you also need to break away from them. There is not a step-by-step formula that will work or a computerized routine that will take away the uncertainty. All you can do is face the next pitcher and do your best. What I'm talking about in this book is a change of stance, perhaps, or of grip or focus, that I believe will add a few points to hitters who are already in the .300 range.

Chapter 15

Consensus and the Sequence of Ideas

The emphasis in this book has been on the power of the single human mind, indeed of the necessity of a single mind, to make its own forecasts. I claim, in fact, that we have no choice in the matter; we cannot turn over the responsibility for forecasting to someone else; when decisions must be made, we are obliged to turn inward, to what we know, to our own view of the future that is always present in our own mind. If in this task we feel naked and inadequate, it is mainly because we have accepted the myth that Someone, Somewhere, must know the Right Answer better than we do. The purpose of this book has been to attack that myth, and thereby to give us a greater sense of confidence, and also to offer techniques that may help us more frequently to beat our competitors.

This emphasis on self-reliance, however, will have gone too far if you believe that I am urging you to abandon all interest in what the majority of other forecasters are doing. To the contrary, I believe that an interest in majority opinion, let's call it loosely the *consensus view,* is quite normal and healthy. The consensus is an important point of reference. But we should be interested in the consensus because it *is* the consensus, not because it will be correct, and not because we should go that way ourselves. Our interest should be, "Which way are most people leaning, and how hard?" "Where is the herd?"

It would be good to know the consensus on several fronts: Where is "the market?" Where is "the consumer?" Where is "the competition?" The problem is that it simply isn't possible to obtain data on all the kinds of consensus that might be useful. There are, however, a few issues that can be reasonably followed. For instance, on the outlook for the national economy, one could obtain data on the following:

1. The Administration's consensus.
2. The consensus of your own staff.
3. The BLUE CHIP Consensus (a private survey of 50 leading economists).

THE ADMINISTRATION'S CONSENSUS

The Administration's consensus is put forth by the Office of Management and Budget (OMB), and is sometimes embellished by the President himself, or by his Council of Economics Advisers or the Treasury. The OMB's outlook would seem to have a high chance of being correct, inasmuch as its authors are very close indeed to the so-called policy variables that frequently spoil otherwise smooth-running economic models. The problem is that the OMB is directly involved in *selling* policy, so its forecasts may reflect action by Congress that the Administration greatly desires. Also, the OMB, because of political pressure, cannot forecast other than a rosy picture. No Administration will forecast that it will lead the country into a recession. Administrations overestimate growth and underestimate deficits. (See Figure 15–1.) The average error of the OMB over the past 15 years in estimating the federal budget deficit has been 125 percent. Business leaders should nonetheless attempt to follow the Administration's forecasts, bearing in mind that those forecasts reflect what is *wished* for rather than what is most likely.

Figure 15–1. The average error of the OMB's forecasts of the federal deficit has been about 125 percent during the last 15 years.

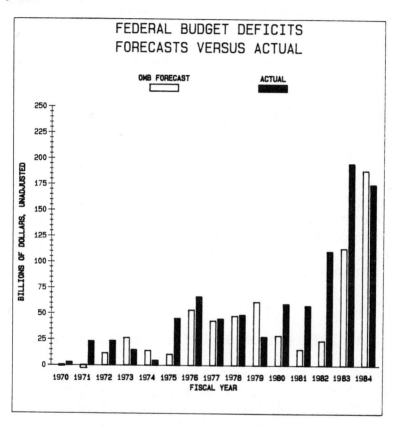

Source: OMB Budget Plan; Joint Economic Committee for actual figures.

STAFF CONSENSUS

The consensus of an executive's own staff is important mainly in terms of communication. It suggests how much effort will be required to sway those people in the direction that the chief executive is leaning. The best way I have found to obtain the consensus of operating staff is to involve them in a group forecasting exercise that mocks a session by some government body; for example, to assemble seven to ten key staff members on the same day that the Open Market Committee of the Federal Reserve meets, and to spend no more than an hour and a half coming to consensus on what the future course of U.S. monetary policy should be. This involves estimating the strength of the economy, the direction of interest rates, the level of inflation, the strength of the dollar, and so on. The setting of the Mock Committee, with a charter to publish a "policy directive to the New York Fed," highlights for the participants the difficulties faced by the Fed itself—it helps them to see that no one has the Right Answer.

PROFESSIONAL PUBLISHED CONSENSUS

The BLUE CHIP Consensus is a private survey taken each month by Robert Eggert, himself formerly a chief economist for a major manufacturing firm. Eggert contacts about 50 bank and corporate economists, along with the major econometric forecasting firms, and gets their opinions about what the future will be, at least in terms of its economic indicators. He then publishes his results, along with an average of what the experts have told him, which he calls the "BLUE CHIP Consensus." Anyone who pays the subscription fee may receive the data.

Several articles have appeared in prestigious journals on the value of consensus forecasts, including the BLUE CHIP. It is argued that (1) a consensus forecast has a better track record than any individual, that (2) a consensus forecast will usually give correctly the direction if not the magnitude of the future economy, and that (3) knowing the direction of change is the thing of most interest to businesspeople. I take issue with all of these points.

First of all, the closer one gets to an eventuality, the more likely that one's forecast of it will be correct. Thus, if you examine a consensus forecast for 1983 GNP in early 1982, you get one thing, and if you examine it again in late 1983, you get another. When the year is almost over, everyone's forecast will start to look pretty good. But for a business leader's forecasts to make money, it has to be righter sooner than the competition's. It has to lead the pack.

Furthermore, I'm not at all sure that knowing the direction is really more important then knowing the magnitude. I have witnessed occasions in an extremely volatile commodities market in which direction by itself can make money, but such "day-trading" is not really parallel with long-term business strategy. Knowing which way to lean is of limited value if you don't know how hard to lean. If you're leaning the wrong way, but you're not leaning too hard, you can recover quickly. I believe that it is the combination of direction and magnitude on which big gains can be made, or big losses incurred.

How accurate is the BLUE CHIP Consensus? Figure 15–2 shows a 24-month history of the BLUE CHIP in forecasting 1983 GNP. Twelve months before the year 1983 began, the BLUE CHIP forecast was for a GNP of 4.1 percent growth over the preceding year. The actual growth figure was 3.7 percent. This may seem pretty good. Notice, however, that over the 24-month course, the direction of opinion changed; it was downward for 12 months, and then upward for the remainder. So the "mood" of the 50 experts was steadily worsening until 1983 actually got started, and then it turned around. Notice also the "range" of the estimate. I have shown this by means of the "Econometric High" each month, and the "Econometric Low." In the case of the 1983 GNP forecast, it is perhaps significant that the "human" estimate, the consensus, was always more accurate than the econometric one. The human consensus saw the change in direction before the economic modellers. However, the humans on Eggert's list probably all use computer models to some extent.

**Figure 15–2. Forecasters, on average, steadily lost confidence
in what 1983 would bring, until the year began — at which
point they changed their minds.**

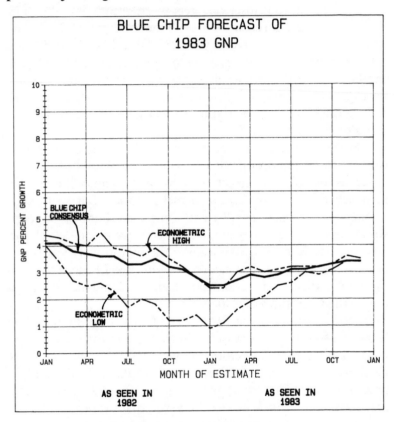

Source: BLUE CHIP Economic Indicators.

Figure 15–3. Although everyone knew there was a "boom" coming, it was halfway over before the consensus really adjusted.

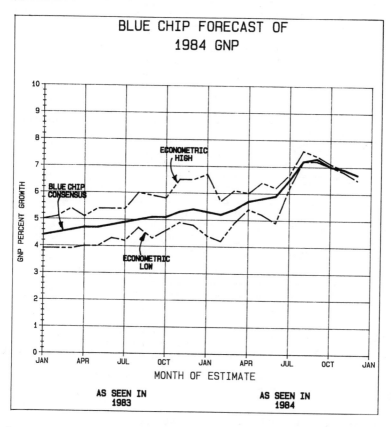

Source: BLUE CHIP Economic Indicators.

Figure 15–4. Forecasters changed their mind five times about the 1985 GNP.

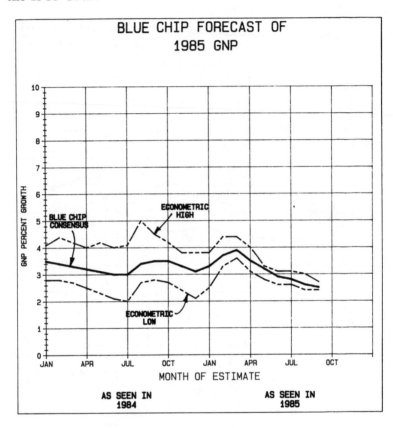

Source: BLUE CHIP Economic Indicators.

Figure 15–3 gives the history, what I call the sequence of ideas, for the BLUE CHIP forecast of 1984 GNP. It begins at 4.4 percent versus a final correct answer of 6.8 percent. The direction all along is upward. Is this then helpful? I doubt it. The thing about 1984 *not* to have missed was the magnitude of the recovery. Virtually everyone knew there was a recovery underway. Virtually no one, including people in the Administration, forecast that it would be the best performance since the 1950s. So the difference between a forecast of 4.4 percent and the final figure of 6.8 percent is like the difference between night and day. If you operated according to the consensus, you missed the biggest boom in three decades of American history.

There is present here a purely mathematical phenomenon that requires careful attention: Two figures, representing rather small percentages, don't ever look very far apart. If you guess 4 percent and the answer is 5 percent, then you say that you didn't miss it by far. But the U.S. GNP, in 1972 dollars, has a full growth range of only about −2 percent to +8 percent. The range, then, is ten percentage points. Your guess of 4 percent when it was actually 5 percent is thus really off by 10 percent of the range. The BLUE CHIP Consensus of 4.4 percent versus the final figure of 6.8 percent represents an underforecast of 55 percent. The math would be as follows:

$$\frac{4.4\% - 6.8\%}{4.4\%} = -0.55$$

Figure 15–4 shows the same thing as the previous two figures, only for the 1985 GNP. There are four changes of direction over 20 months. If, 18 months ahead of the fact, the BLUE CHIP Consensus was omniscient, and if you happened to have been subscribing to the low econometric forecast, you would be 33 percent too conservative; if, on the other hand, you happened to be subscribing to the high econometric forecast, you would be 33 percent too expansive.

CONCLUSION

The message is that attempting to follow various kinds of consensus forecasts, and especially the sequence of their estimates, may be a useful way of judging how you stand. But no individual forecaster, much less a consensus, will ever predict the surprises on which the real world turns. The consensus did not predict OPEC, nor the demise of OPEC. The consensus did not predict Volcker's tight money policy, nor its release. The consensus did not predict the Reagan GNP boom, nor its stagnation. Nor did any individual forecaster predict any of the above, especially in terms both of direction and magnitude (and especially when one recognizes that 4 is actually "10 percent" different from 5).

Readers interested in strengthening their own objectivity will make their own forecast first, using their knowledge of history in the ways described earlier. They will then try to determine where the herd is. Finally, they will deliberately seek out contrary views—they will not read only analysts who confirm their own optimism or pessimism. They will continuously submit their view to the test of reason and, of course, willy-nilly, to the final test of the market.

Chapter 16

Conclusion

"Your adversary is never completely wrong."
Professor Noel Stock
The University of Toledo

Because the forecasts of economists are wrong, are not improving, and are not likely to improve, business leaders should consider whether they can conduct their affairs more profitably without economists. In one alternative approach, given in this book, decisionmakers put more trust in themselves and are supported in somewhat new ways by their researchers. Quantitative, narrative, and critical history are suggested as the foundation of strategic analysis, along with systematic monitoring of the front page and a stricture to promote verbal clarity and to prohibit graphic distortion.

The final judge of any approach, with or without economists, should be the market. Measure any advice against (1) how much it increases profits and (2) how much it assures longevity for the firm. Examine whether "psychological comfort" is your reason for continuing to pay economists, despite the lack of results on your bottom line.

No one knows the Right Answers. Truth cannot be determined. But what matters in business is to come closer to it than one's competitors, and to do so ahead of them. The implication of this, in an age of increasing uncertainty, is to devise strategies that permit step-like, modular investment—so that as systematic monitoring reveals change, you can adapt your strategies faster than your competitors adapt theirs.

In the opening chapter of this book I indicated that many readers, seeing the book's title, would be sympathetic to my thesis. It is a subject whose time has arrived. The public acknowledgment that the professional applications of economics can and should be severely challenged will be all that is needed for many pragmatic businesspeople to make changes in their approach. The groundwork is already laid in the failure of forecasting.

"Economist jokes" abound, and even economists tell them. Recently, at a trade fair in which I participated, I heard one of my fellow panelists respond to the moderator as follows: "I'm going to say something as an economist, and then I'm going to say something practical." We all laughed politely. We may not take these jokes seriously today, but it probably won't be long before we do. (As it turned out, my colleague did not keep his promise; he did indeed say things as an economist, but then he stopped. Nothing practical came out. It was a double joke on him, but of course he didn't get it.) I think the existence of such jokes are prophetic. At some point they will cease to be funny, especially for the profession itself.

Another way of saying this is to acknowledge, strongly, that I am not the only one who has arrived at conclusions such as the ones in this book. Here is additional confirmation from other sources:

1. "Dissatisfaction with current forecasting stems from an expectation of certainty that cannot be fulfilled. Firms cannot predict the future, but they can plan and be prepared for it." (From "Oil Prices: Living with the Perils of Prophecy," *Petroleum Intelligence Weekly*, December 3, 1984.)
2. "The idea that 'true wisdom lies in the masterful administration of the unforeseen' encapsulates my feelings about leadership." (Sir Trevor Holdswith, chairman of the British engineering firm of Guest Keen and Nettlefolds, in *Chief Executives View Their Jobs*, The Conference Board, New York, 1985.)

3. "Business is reality testing." (Dr. James E. Tillotson, vice president of research, Oceanspray Cranberries, at The Federal Reserve Bank of Kansas City's Conference on Agricultural Policy, September 1985.)
4. "Economics has no universally accepted laws. Each forecasting team builds a model around its own beliefs about how the economy ticks. Even if two models are identical, their forecasts can still differ. Different forecasters feed in different assumptions about things like government policy and world trade. And, because equations can never fully explain the past behaviour of variables, there is scope for 'massaging' the final results. When weathermen make forecasts they at least know whether it is raining or sunny today, but economic forecasters have to start by predicting the immediate past. It will be ages before they will know if they were right about even this, because published data are subject to frequent and large revisions." (Author, "Better than a Blindfold and a Pin," *The Economist,* November, 1985.)

This passage sounds so much like what I have said in this book that one is bound to wonder how it could appear in the "heart" of the economists' home territory, *The Economist* magazine itself. Have economists suddenly come clean? The answer is, "Definitely not." The passage was taken from an article called, "Better than a Blindfold and a Pin." This title was evidently supplied by the editor, not the author, for no mention of such a thesis—that economic models are better than darts on the wall—is made in the article. In fact, the author concludes with, "Today's 'best buy' in economic models could become tomorrow's forecasting disaster. Success can be a matter of luck. Even a stopped watch is correct twice a day." The prevailing convention, which the editor confirmed by supplying a gratuitous title, is to ignore the obvious. Economics is still widely believed to be a science that over time will yield Truth.

If you challenge someone with a Ph.D. in aeronautical engineering to prove the worth of that discipline, he has the option of taking you on a plane ride to Atlanta, or a spaceship to the moon. If you challenge someone with a Ph.D. in ocular physiology, she has the option of mending your retina with a laser. But if you challenge someone with a Ph.D. in economics, he is offended. You have broken convention. You are being irreverent.

Suppose you do issue such a challenge to an economist, as I have done from time to time, at a person-to-person level. You'll smack right up against a stone wall. You might be asked, "Have you studied the principles of economics, as I have, for eight years?" The defense is that you don't understand, because you don't understand. Arguments that would prove the case in favor of economics cannot be made to you, because they are too technical; the principles require years of study; the principles require advanced mathematics. If you haven't paid your dues, then it's no surprise that you don't understand.

Furthermore, to an economist, it is not surprising that when the principles of economics are discussed, the phenomenon of "economic circularity" sets in. From his point of view, this is what to expect when amateurs tackle something they don't understand. The inside term for this is *"Wall Street Journal"* economics, referring to the perils associated with trying to explain things to the public. A professional economist will not discover truth in the popular debate over economics, but rather in the empirical analysis of data. The expression of new-found truth is couched in the language of advanced statistics. Those who cannot speak this language will forever be excluded. Advanced research and advanced findings are for the benefit of other researchers; that the public cannot benefit, because of the translation problem, is lamentable perhaps, but in no way a weakness of the science of economics itself.

Although I have spoken several times about engaging at a philosophical level in the battle over whether economists have failed or not, it is really at the practical level that my argument rests. If the forecasts were right, who would care what language the forecasters spoke? Who would care about their reasons? After all, in business, it's much more important to be right, than to be right for the right reasons. But since the forecasts are wrong, why must we continue to have faith in a body of reasoning that we can neither speak nor penetrate without years and years of effort? Since the forecasts are wrong, isn't the only remaining appeal left that of helpful explanation of intermediary principles? It seems to me that using plain language is crucial. If a theory is only communicable between specialists, then you go by their results; if those results are nonproductive, you ignore them. For the intermediary principles of the specialists to be useful, they must be expressed in plain language. Here is a quote from the oil industry, which is the industry perhaps most imperiled by the specialists:

> Forecasting has reached a highly refined state, and there is little reason to expect meaningful improvements. But making the process transparent to executives—so they understand how the assumptions are made and how they depend on one another—is a first step toward improving the planning process.[1]

To this recommendation, I would add that the dimensions of forecasting be enlarged. In the case of oil, for instance, how can forecasting proceed without knowledge along the dimension of religion? Who owns most of the world's reserves? Answer: Islam. Why is there a crisis in the Persian Gulf? Answer: Islam. Why did OPEC launch one of the largest and potentially most damaging attack on Western civilization in the last several centuries? Answer: Islam.

Likewise, how can forecasting proceed without knowledge of national security issues, such as the conflict between the United States and the Soviet Union? How much business depends on this conflict? Answer: Trillions of dollars.

More money can be made if businessleaders enlarge their scope. Figure 16-1 shows a simplistic diagram of what the "average" businessperson brings to a job. He or she has mastered virtually all the elementary quantitative principles needed and has slightly more ability in "advanced quantitative" reasoning than in "advanced qualitative." Economists try to pull people toward more advanced quantitative approaches. I am urging the alternative, and suggest using better qualitative techniques.

I do not expect in this book to have made an air-tight case. Many openings will be found for criticism. One of the most helpful things for me to keep in mind has been the aphorism, "Your adversary is never completely wrong." This goes for me as well as for my critics.

Figure 16-1. Growth in the direction of elementary qualitative reasoning is of more value to businesspersons than growth toward even the most advanced quantitative reasoning.

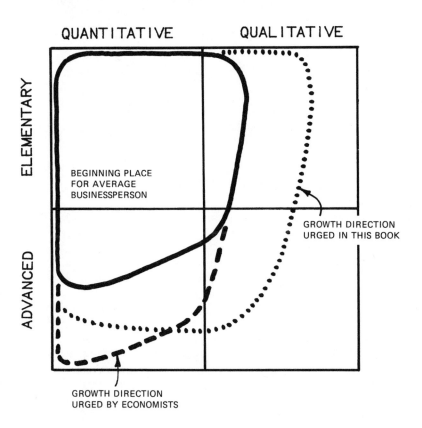

BUSINESS REASONING

QUANTITATIVE   QUALITATIVE

ELEMENTARY

BEGINNING PLACE
FOR AVERAGE
BUSINESSPERSON

GROWTH DIRECTION
URGED IN THIS BOOK

ADVANCED

GROWTH DIRECTION
URGED BY ECONOMISTS

Epilog:

Government Without Economists?

The linchpin of my argument in favor of business without economists is that chief executives can set the standards for judgment. They can look at their bottom line and their firm's chances for longevity, and decide what kind of expert advice has the most profitable results.

No such linchpin is apparent in the case of "government without economists." There is no easy standard for judging when government is serving better, or serving worse. My grandfather might have said that the reduced role of government when he was young was better; I may say that the U.S. government's role is not so bad today, compared with other countries I've seen. A Frenchman, an Englishman, or others may disagree.

There is also an important sense in which business needs its antithesis, which is government. The pages of history confirm the course of unrestrained human greed—in business monopoly, child labor, slavery. If competition is the elemental core of business, it is probably best that it be subject to rules. The senior partner of my own company is fond of saying, "A good game is better with a good referee." What other tools does such a referee have, if not central planning? How else to do central planning if not by econometrics?

The odds against running a government without economists would have seemed to me astronomical, had it not happened in my lifetime that a President tried to abolish his own
Council of Economic Advisers (CEA). Why did this effort of
President Reagan's fail? I have no inside knowledge, but my
suppositions would be as follows:

1. There was no clear signal from business that abolishing
   the CEA would be desirable. The convention in business
   is to pay large sums for economic forecasts that are
   always wrong.
2. The White House directs the enforcement of laws, many
   of which have been framed with the help of, and the legal
   necessity of using, econometric analysis. How can the
   White House do its job unless it has its own specialists to
   argue with the thousands of economic specialists already
   entrenched throughout the bureaucracy?
3. Many countries in the world are run by central planners.
   How can good communication take place if the White
   House doesn't have its own experts—in fact doesn't have
   the *leading* experts?

It should also be pointed out that business, in order to lobby
most effectively, may need its own economists. Nowhere in this
book is it argued that they all be summarily dismissed; rather, it
is suggested that they shift toward a different kind of lieutenancy
for their chiefs. Even a marginal shift might produce handsome
results for those few institutions that do it.

In the case of national regulation, econometric-style planning is already a part of history; it can't be abolished. In the
international case, things are not completely formed as yet,
especially in the less-developed countries (LDCs). Assistance in
designing government structures for LDCs is called "development economics." At the 25th anniversary of the Center for
Economic Development of Williams College, in Williamstown,
Massachusetts, in late October of 1985, a debate took place
among the leaders of this field. According to a report by Leonard
Silk in *The New York Times:*

Development economics is in crisis, because it failed to foresee the severe imbalance in many countries in the 1980s and cannot point a credible way out, [said the majority]. Gerald M. Meier of Stanford University blamed economics itself for being overly formal and mathematical, for abstracting unduly from the institutions, organizational framework and conflicts that are inherent in development problems. Among the topics suggested for greater study were statistics, communication skills, study of the policy-making process, philosophy, especially the ethical issues involved for professional economists working with or for politicians, and what was referred to as "ordinary knowledge" that could be gained only from experience.[1]

That the economists in government need more "ordinary knowledge," including ordinary knowledge of the marketplace, seems to me unquestionable. Not too long ago, an economist working for the Department of Transportation called me, he said, to check his opinion on the importance of toll increases on the Saint Lawrence Seaway. He said he could not see how the proposed toll increase could make much of a difference to traffic out on the Great Lakes, because the increase was only about 5 cents per bushel. I did not know where to begin. The man was missing "ordinary knowledge." He was apparently thinking that 5 cents was small against the price of a bushel, which might be $2.50 for corn, or $3.50 for wheat. But those of us in the market know that the annual variation of price is much smaller—usually less than 50 cents. So he was proposing that a penalty of 5 cents, 10 percent of the range of price variation, would not make a difference. I told him that *one* cent was enough to route things down another channel, and that sometimes one-quarter of a cent would do it. I thought but didn't say that he was off by an order of magnitude. He was not satisfied with my response. He wanted to know if studies had been made to prove what I had told him. And unless I wanted to give up and take another regulatory "hit" in profits, I would produce such a study.

Most if not all business leaders have had similar experiences. It becomes not so much a hope for "government without economists" as a hope for "government with *better* economists." How can a referee be good who's never played the game? How can we expect to take college professors directly into high government positions and urge them to advance the cause of mankind, when they have never tested their views in the market itself?

It is idle to hope for government without economists, and it is probably unwise. But it may be worth lobbying for better referees, for economic appointees who have more "ordinary knowledge."

List of Figures

Notes

Chapter 2

1. Peter F. Drucker, "The Changed World Economy," *Foreign Affairs*, Spring 1986, pp. 768–791.
2. *Petroleum Intelligence Weekly*, Monthly Supplement, December 10, 1984.
3. Drucker, *op. cit.*, p. 768.

Chapter 3

1. Drucker, *op. cit.*, p. 768.

Chapter 4

1. Edward Cowan, "U.S. Revising G.N.P. of 1977, Adds 3% Growth," *The New York Times*, July 21, 1984.
2. Henry Kaufman, "Kaufman Says 'Orthodoxy of Monetarism' Will Probably Be Replaced," Commodity News Service, June 6, 1985.
3. Joel Garreau, *Nine Nations of America* (Boston: Houghton Mifflin, 1981).

Chapter 6

1. Beryl W. Sprinkel, as quoted in William Gruber, "Sprinkel Sees Economic Growth Spurt," *Chicago Tribune*, October 13, 1985.

Chapter 7

1. John Henry Newman, *An Essay in Aid of a Grammar of Assent,* London: Longmans, Green & Co., 1924, pp. 360, 361.
2. *Ibid.*

Chapter 8

1. Ad from Bipartisan Budget Appeal, "Budget Cuts Now, Then Tax Reform," *The New York Times,* June 23, 1985.

Chapter 10

1. From Charles L. Mee, Jr., *The Marshall Plan* (New York: Simon & Schuster, 1984).
2. *Ibid.,* p. 79.
3. *Ibid.,* p. 97.
4. *Ibid.,* p. 84.
5. *Ibid.,* p. 88.
6. *Ibid.,* p. 230.

Chapter 14

1. George Orwell, "In Front of Your Nose," *The Collected Essays, Journalism and Letters of George Orwell* (New York: Harcourt Brace Jovanovich, 1968) Volume 4, p. 125.
2. Orwell, "Politics and the English Language," *Ibid.,* p. 136.
3. Michael Quint, "Economy Gives Alternating Signals," *The New York Times,* October 14, 1985.
4. A. Terry Bahill, "Take Your Eye Off the Ball, Scientist Coaches Sluggers," *The New York Times,* June 12, 1984.

Chapter 16

1. "Oil Prices: Living with the Perils of Prophecy," *Petroleum Intelligence Weekly,* December 3, 1984, p. 7.

Epilog

1. Leonard Silk, "Economic Scene: New Thinking on Poor Lands," *The New York Times,* November 6, 1985.

Index